Collins

GCSE 9-1
Religious Studies

Revision Guide

Dan Phillips and Rob Phillips

About this Revision & Practice book

Revise

These pages provide a recap of key concepts for Christianity, Catholicism, Islam, Judaism and Sikhism, and for other GCSE topics.

You should read through all the information before taking the Quick Test at the end. This will test whether you can recall the key facts.

Quick Test

1. Who can lead Christian worship?
2. When does the Jumu'ah occur and who leads it?
3. Outline what usually happens during worship in a synagogue.

Practise

These topic-based questions appear shortly after the revision pages for each topic and will test whether you have understood the topic. If you get any of the questions wrong, make sure you read the correct answer carefully.

Review

These topic-based questions appear later in the book, allowing you to revisit the topic and test how well you have remembered the information. If you get any of the questions wrong, make sure you read the correct answer carefully.

Mix it Up

These pages feature a mix of topic-based questions. They will make sure you can recall the relevant information to answer a question on selected topics.

Test Yourself on the Go

Visit our website at **collins.co.uk/collinsGCSErevision** and print off a set of flashcards. These pocket-sized cards feature questions and answers so that you can test yourself on all the key facts anytime and anywhere. You will also find lots more information about the advantages of spaced practice and how to plan for it.

Workbook

This section features even more topic-based questions as well as practice exam papers, providing two further practice opportunities to guarantee the best results.

Practice exam papers to help you prepare for Edexcel GCSE Religious Studies are available at **collins.co.uk/collinsGCSErevision**

ebook

To access the ebook revision guide visit

collins.co.uk/ebooks

and follow the step-by-step instructions.

Contents

Review Questions

Recap of KS3 Key Concepts: Christianity

1 Where was Jesus born? [1]

2 Where did Jesus live? [1]

3 Who were Jesus' parents? [1]

4 Who visited Him after his birth? [1]

5 What gifts were given? [3]

6 Who baptised Him? [1]

7 Where was Jesus baptised? [1]

8 What happened when Jesus came out of the water? [2]

9 How long was Jesus tested in the wilderness? [1]

10 Name one of the temptations. [1]

11 How many disciples did Jesus call? [1]

12 What does 'Peter' mean? [1]

13 What does 'Messiah' mean? [1]

14 What is a parable? [1]

15 What did Jesus teach about forgiveness? [1]

16 What is meant by the term 'heaven'? [1]

17 What did Jesus teach about how to treat others? [1]

18 What is a miracle? [1]

19 Name one of the three main types of miracle. [1]

20 What happened at the Last Supper? [3]

21 Where did the Last Supper take place? [1]

Review Questions

22 Who betrayed Jesus? [1]

23 How did Jesus die? [1]

24 Who was killed with Jesus? [1]

25 Where was Jesus' body placed? [1]

26 What is the resurrection of Jesus? [1]

27 Who discovered the empty tomb? [1]

28 What name did Jesus usually use for God? [1]

29 Where do Christians worship? [1]

30 What is a pulpit? [1]

31 What is a lectern? [1]

32 What is a font? [1]

33 What is an altar? [1]

34 What is the name of the Christian holy book? [1]

....

35 What are the two parts of the book called? [1]

....

36 Explain the nature and practice of prayer. [3]

....

....

....

37 How do Christians worship? [1]

....

38 Why do Christians study the Bible? [1]

....

39 What takes place during the Christian birth rites? [5]

....

....

....

....

40 What takes place during the Christian death rites? [3]

....

....

....

Total Marks .... / 53

Review Questions

Recap of KS3 Key Concepts: Islam

1 Name the founder of Islam. [1]

2 When did he live? [1]

3 Name his wife. [1]

4 Who visited him in the cave? [1]

5 What are the 'recitations'? [1]

6 When did he migrate to Medina? [1]

7 Name the main city of Islam. [1]

8 What is the Arabic name Muslims use for God? [1]

9 Where do Muslims worship? [1]

10 When do main prayers take place? [1]

11 What must Muslims do before worshipping? [3]

....

....

....

12 What is a minaret? [1]

....

13 What is the name of the Muslim holy book? [1]

....

14 In which language is the Muslim holy book written? [1]

....

15 Explain how Muslims perform Salah (prayer). [4]

....

....

....

....

16 How do Muslims worship? [1]

....

17 Why do Muslims study the scriptures? [1]

....

18 What happens in the Aqeeqah ceremony? [4]

....

....

....

....

Total Marks .... / 26

Review Questions

Recap of KS3 Key Concepts: Judaism

1 Who founded the Jewish nation? [1]

2 Who led the Israelites out of Egypt? [1]

3 What is the Exodus? [1]

4 How did they leave Egypt? [1]

5 Where were the Ten Commandments given? [1]

6 On what were the Ten Commandments 'written'? [1]

7 What is the Jewish name for God? [1]

8 Where do Jews worship? [1]

9 What is the Jewish holy day? [1]

10 Where are the scrolls kept? [1]

11 What is a bimah? [1]

12 What is the 'ner tamid'? [1]

....

13 What is a minyan? [2]

....

....

14 What is the name of the Jewish holy book? [1]

....

15 In what language is the Jewish holy book written? [1]

....

16 Explain the nature and practice of prayer. [3]

....

....

....

17 How do Jews worship? [3]

....

....

....

18 What takes place during the Jewish birth rites? [4]

....

....

....

....

Total Marks .... / 26

Review Questions

Recap of KS3 Key Concepts: Sikhism

1 Who was the first Guru? [1]

2 When did the first Guru live? [1]

3 Who was the last Guru? [1]

4 When did the last Guru live? [1]

5 What is the 'Khalsa'? [1]

6 How many 'beloved ones' were there? [1]

7 How many human Gurus were there? [1]

8 What are the Five Ks? [5]

9 Where do Sikhs worship? [1]

10 When do Sikhs worship? [1]

....

11 What is a takht? [1]

....

12 Who is the 'Granthi'? [1]

....

13 What is 'Kara Parshad'? [1]

....

14 What is the name of the Sikh holy book? [1]

....

15 How do Sikhs worship? [4]

....

....

....

....

16 Why do Sikhs read the scriptures? [1]

....

17 What takes place during the Sikh birth rites? [3]

....

....

....

Total Marks .... / 26

Who is God?

You must be able to:

- Explore the nature of God
- Investigate the origins of the Trinity in the Bible.

Key Scripture and Religious Teaching

In Matthew 28:19, Jesus commands the apostles: 'Go therefore and make disciples of all nations, baptising them in the name of the Father and of the Son and of the Holy Spirit'.

The Trinity in the Bible

- The word Trinity does not occur in the Bible.
- The Bible teaches that there is one God.
- Old Testament, Deuteronomy 6:4, 'Hear, O Israel: The Lord our God, the Lord is one'.
- While writing about idols in the New Testament, St Paul says: '... we know that "An idol is nothing at all in the world" and that "There is no God but one"' (1 Corinthians 8:4).
- God is infinitely greater than we are and beyond our understanding.
- God can be described as being omnipotent, omniscient, omnipresent, omnibenevolent and eternal (see page 39).
- Christian scripture teaches that the Father is God, that Jesus is God and that the Holy Spirit is God.
- He is one God existing in three 'persons'.
- He is the triune God: three coexistent, coeternal 'persons' who make up one God.
- The relationship between the 'persons' of the Trinity is a mystery.
- In John 14:16–17, Jesus says: 'And I will ask the Father, and he will give you another advocate [counsellor] to help you and be with you forever – the Spirit of truth.'
- Jesus the Christ, together with the Father and the Holy Spirit are known as the Trinity.
- God reveals Himself in three expressions: the Creator of all things, the Saviour and the Life-Giving Spirit.
- The individual 'persons' of the Trinity have different tasks.

Key Point

The Bible teaches that there is one God.

The Father

- The Father is the ultimate origin of the universe.
- He and the Word created all things.

- He is the universe's source and cause: Genesis 1:1, 'In the beginning God created the heavens and the earth'.
- In 1 Corinthians 8:6, St Paul writes: '… yet for us there is but one God, the Father, from whom all things came and for whom we live'.

The Son

- The Son is involved in the creation and maintenance of the universe: 1 Corinthians 8:6, '… and there is but one Lord, Jesus Christ, through whom all things came and through whom we live'.
- John 1:1, 'In the beginning was the Word, and the Word was with God, and the Word was God'. Here the term 'Word' is a title given to Jesus.
- Christians believe that Jesus perfectly revealed the Father: John 14:7, 'If you really know me, you will know my Father as well. From now on, you do know him and have seen him'.
- The Son's work is in salvation: Matthew 1:21, 'She will give birth to a son, and you are to give him the name Jesus, because he will save his people from their sins'.
- The Father works through the Son, who functions as His agent.

The Holy Spirit

- The Spirit was involved in the creation and maintenance of the universe: Genesis 1:2, 'Now the earth was formless and empty, darkness was over the surface of the deep, and the Spirit of God was hovering over the waters'.
- He is the agent of divine revelation: Ephesians 3:5, '… it has now been revealed by the Spirit to God's holy apostles and prophets'.
- He sanctifies: 1 Peter 1:2, '… who have been chosen according to the foreknowledge of God the Father, through the sanctifying work of the Spirit, to be obedient to Jesus Christ and sprinkled with his blood'.
- He enabled the work of Jesus: Acts 10:38, '… how God anointed Jesus of Nazareth with the Holy Spirit and power and how he went around doing good and healing all who were under the power of the devil, because God was with him'.
- The Father works by the power of the Holy Spirit.

Key Point

Scripture teaches that the Father is God, that Jesus is God and that the Holy Spirit is God.

Quick Test

1. What does the word 'Trinity' mean?
2. Who are the three 'persons' in the Trinity?
3. What is the Father's role in the Trinity?
4. What is the main work of the Son?
5. What does the Spirit do?

Key Words

Trinity
coexistent
Christ
revelation
sanctify

What Makes Jesus Special?

You must be able to:

- Understand Jesus as the Word of God made flesh
- Examine the purpose of His mortal life and His example
- Explore His last days (The Passion), the Resurrection and the Ascension.

Key Scripture and Religious Teaching

John 1:1, 'In the beginning was the Word, and the Word was with God, and the Word was God.'

John 1:14, 'The Word became flesh and made his dwelling among us.'

Jesus, the Word

- John 1:1 refers to Jesus as 'the Word' and verse 14 says He 'became flesh':
  - The Greek for 'the Word' is 'logos', and this was used to denote the creative force, as well as logic and reason.
  - In the Old Testament, 'the Word of God' often referred to the way in which God communicated with His people.
  - John combines these two concepts in relation to Jesus.
- Matthew and Luke record His miraculous birth to a virgin, Mary.
- Joseph intended to finish their relationship but Matthew's Gospel tells us that he was dissuaded in a dream.
- The Magi (Wise Men) followed a star to Bethlehem, while angels told a group of shepherds about Jesus' birth.
- King Herod tried to have the baby Jesus killed but the family escaped to Egypt.
- Little is known of His early life as the son of a carpenter apart from a visit to Jerusalem when He was 12.

Key Point

A variety of unusual events, including stars, angels, shepherds and wise men, accompanied Jesus' birth.

His Mortal Life and Example

- Jesus' public ministry began when he was about 30.
- He was baptised, by full immersion, in the River Jordan by his cousin John.
- He spent 40 days and 40 nights in the desert being tempted.
- He called 12 disciples to follow and learn from Him. There were fishermen, a tax-collector, even a Zealot.
- All four Gospels have records of Jesus' teaching (e.g. the Sermon on the Mount, parables, the 'I am' sayings, etc.).
- His miracles fall into three main categories: healing miracles and exorcisms, nature miracles and resurrections.
- He taught His followers about the Kingdom of God and the nature of His Messiahship, and Christians try to live in accordance with His teaching and example.

Jesus' Last Days

- After about three years of ministry, Jesus and His disciples went to Jerusalem for Passover.
- He entered the city on a donkey and was popularly welcomed.
- He cleansed the Temple (His Father's House).
- The last days were spent teaching in the Temple Courts and healing.
- The religious authorities plotted to have Him arrested and tried and, following a Roman trial, put to death under the authority of Pontius Pilate.
- Jesus and the disciples ate their last supper together.
- The bread and wine are recalled in the Eucharist.
- They went to pray in the Garden of Gethsemane.
- Judas betrayed Jesus to the authorities with a kiss.
- After several illegal trials, Jesus was sentenced to death.
- He was crucified on what became known as Good Friday.
- Christians believe that Jesus died so that sins could be forgiven.
- His body was placed in a tomb and a stone rolled in front of it.

The Resurrection and the Ascension

- The following Sunday morning His body was gone.
- Peter and some of the women examined the empty tomb, but only the grave clothes remained.
- The authorities claimed that the disciples stole the body.
- The Gospels record many accounts of people who claimed to have met with Jesus after the resurrection.
- Christians call this Sunday, Easter Day.
- After the resurrection, Jesus remained on Earth, teaching the disciples, for 40 days.
- Jesus led them to the vicinity of Bethany (Mount of Olives) where He ascended into heaven (called the ascension).
- Two men in white told the disciples Jesus would come again.

Redemption

- The word 'redemption' means to 'buy back' or 'reclaim'.
- When a slave was bought out of slavery, they were 'redeemed'.
- When Jesus died on the cross, Christians believe that His death purchased believers from slavery to sin and its consequences.
- His death pays the price of a ransom, freeing believers from bondage to sin and death and releasing them to freedom and new life.
- Paul sums this up when writing to Christians in Ephesus (Ephesians 1:7–8).

Quick Test

1. Explain what 'logos' means to Greeks and Jews.
2. Why was Jesus' birth special?
3. What happened to Jesus after his baptism?
4. What are the three main types of miracle?
5. What happened at the resurrection?

Key Point

Christians believe that Jesus' crucifixion made it possible for those who repent of their sins to be forgiven.

Key Point

The resurrection is central to the Christian faith.

Key Words

logos
disciple
Zealot
parable
Passover
Eucharist
resurrection
ascension
redemption

Is Death a Comma or a Full Stop?

You must be able to:

- Understand the difference between biblical and doctrinal views on life after death
- Explain the nature of resurrection, judgement, heaven, hell and purgatory
- Describe the different elements of the funeral rite of passage.

Key Scripture and Religious Teaching

John 11:25, 'Jesus said to her, "I am the resurrection and the life. The one who believes in me will live, even though they die."'

John 14:6, 'Jesus answered, "I am the way and the truth and the life. No one comes to the Father except through me."'

Jewish Funerals

- Soon after a Jew's death, the body is prepared for burial and someone remains with the body.
- Burial should occur as soon as possible.
- An open coffin is only used if the law requires it to be, as the body is wrapped in a kittel (linen cloth).
- Donation or removal of organs is forbidden, as is cremation.
- Many funerals take place in the synagogue and are then followed by a set period of mourning (seven days), known as Shiva.

Christian Funerals

- Christian funerals usually take place about a week after a person dies.
- Many services feature hymns and prayers and often include readings from John 11:25 and Psalm 23.
- Family members are also likely to speak during the service.
- Christians can either be buried or cremated.

Muslim Funerals

- Where possible, the Shahadah (see page 50) is recited before death.
- A member of the family of the same sex washes and wraps the body in white robes, within hours of the death.
- As soon as possible, the body is buried in a grave, with the right side and the head facing Mecca.
- Further prayers are said while people stand beside the grave and once the body is in the ground. Then three days of mourning begin.
- Cremation is forbidden.

> ### Key Point
>
> All religions mark the end of life with the rite of passage of a funeral to symbolise the end of this life and the beginning of the next.

Sikh Funerals

- When a Sikh seems about to die, their family will say the Hymn of Peace at the bedside.
- After death, the body is washed in a yogurt bath before being dressed in new clothes and the **Five Ks**.
- The Ardas (see page 27) is declared before cremation and family members may also share a few words and further prayers.
- A short service may take place in the Gurdwara after the service.
- If the funeral is near to the River Ganges, the ashes will be scattered there; if not, a nearby river will be visited.

The Afterlife

- All of the four religions mentioned above believe that life continues after death.
- Jews, Christians and Muslims all believe that death brings judgement before each human's fate is decided.
- For Christians and Jews, entry to **heaven** allows an eternity with God, whereas **hell** provides an eternity without Him.
- In addition, Catholics believe in purgatory, which provides an opportunity to enter heaven even after judgement.
- Some Muslims believe eventually, after punishment, even the sinful will enter paradise (heaven). Others believe some sins are unforgivable.

> **Key Point**
>
> Our life on Earth allows us to learn about God and determines where we spend eternity.

Reincarnation

- Sikhs believe in the cycle of rebirth, with the soul reincarnated in another body at death.
- Their karma (that is their good or bad actions) in their previous life will affect this **reincarnation**.
- If a Sikh lives in a way which produces good karma, they believe they can progress.
- The aim of reincarnation is to achieve 'mukti' (release from rebirth) and be united with God.

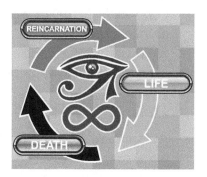

Points to Consider

- Consider:
    - why the question of cremation is a problem for some faiths;
    - why organ donation can be an issue for some believers;
    - why different faiths have different views of when 'the soul' leaves the body;
    - why suicide can be a problem for some faiths.

> **Quick Test**
>
> 1. Outline the differences in Jewish, Christian, Muslim and Sikh attitudes towards cremation.
> 2. Describe the nature of reincarnation and how it can guide the life of a Sikh.

> **Key Words**
>
> funeral
> Five Ks
> heaven
> hell
> reincarnation

How Are We Judged After Death?

You must be able to:

- Describe the Christian beliefs and Church teachings about life after death
- Understand the immortality of the soul in relation to the nature of resurrection, judgement, heaven, hell and purgatory
- Outline other religious beliefs about the afterlife.

> **Key Scripture and Religious Teaching**
>
> Exodus 20:1–17, The Ten Commandments Matthew 5:3–12, The Beatitudes

What is Sin?

- Some Christians believe God will judge them at the end of this life. This judgement will decide their fate in eternity and will take account of the sins they have committed and how they have followed God's will for their lives.
- In religious terms, all of us commit sins but only a few commit crimes, with a sin being an action or thought that contradicts the teachings of a religion, whilst crimes are actions against the laws of the country or state.
- Convicted criminals are punished here on Earth, whereas sins are judged after this life (but may also receive an earthly punishment).
- Some UK laws have their origins in the Ten Commandments, a set of biblical principles which play a key role in Judaism and Christianity.

What Awaits Christians in the Afterlife?

- Accounts such as near-death experiences (NDE) and sightings of ghosts can create arguments about the afterlife.
- For Christians, scripture provides an assurance of an afterlife, either with God or separated from Him.
- Jesus said that he was the 'resurrection and the life' and that all 'who believe in me will live, even though they die' (John 11:25f).
- John 3:16: 'God so loved the world that he gave his one and only Son, that whoever believes in him shall not perish but have eternal life'.
- These scriptures created the central Christian belief that Jesus conquered death by rising from the dead after His crucifixion. This means that anyone who accepts Jesus as Lord and Saviour has the hope of this afterlife.
- Heaven allows for an eternity with God, whereas hell creates an eternity without Him.
- Whilst many Christians believe there will be a physical resurrection, some Christians believe that, as human souls will not need a physical body in the afterlife, heaven and hell may not be physical places but spiritual ones.

Key Point

Christian teaching suggests that hell was created for Lucifer and other fallen angels. God had created Lucifer as the perfect angel but he was thrown out of heaven for becoming proud of his own glory and seeking the praise of other angels.

Key Point

The afterlife allows our souls to live on when our physical bodies have died.

- Many Roman Catholics believe in purgatory, which is an in-between state of cleansing and preparation for heaven for those who are not automatically received into heaven or condemned to hell.
- Christians believe that this world will end when Jesus returns from heaven to bring the resurrection of the dead and the final judgement (the Second Coming or the Parousia).

How Will Muslims Be Judged?

- During the Day of Resurrection, all will be judged to spend an eternity in paradise or in hell.
- Paradise ('the Garden' – Jannah) is a place of physical and spiritual pleasure.
- Hell (Jahannam) is a place of physical and spiritual suffering, with seven levels of a fiery crater, the lowest of which contains a cauldron of burning pitch reserved for the worst offenders.
- As Allah is just and merciful, Muslims believe that all sins can be repented of with the exception of refusing to worship Allah, which can never be forgiven.
- Some Muslims believe that paradise awaits those who lose their lives in Jihad (holy war), including suicide bombers; however, others point out that suicide is forbidden in Islam and, consequently, suicide bombers will go to hell.

Jewish Beliefs

- The Torah clearly emphasises the present and contains little of the overt belief in heaven or hell.
- Consequently, an Orthodox Jew may believe that the souls of the righteous dead go to heaven or remain in limbo until the Messiah comes to resurrect them.
- Wicked souls could be destroyed at death or spend eternity being tormented by demons.

How Can Life Be Reborn?

- Sikhs believe that human life is the later stages of the soul's progress towards becoming one with God, following the cycle of birth, life, death and rebirth (reincarnation).
- Although the body dies, the soul is immortal and, at death, moves on to the next stage of existence.
- The soul of a good person will find favour in the next life but that of an evil person will continue in the unending cycle of birth and death.
- A Sikh will strive during each life for 'mukti', the concept of the emancipation (setting free) of the soul from the cycle of rebirth.

 Key Point

All religions believe that our actions are judged at the end of our lives, whether we enter heaven or hell or are reborn.

 Key Words

sin
Jannah
Jahannam
Messiah

Quick Test

1. Describe what purgatory is.
2. How are Christians judged when they die?

How Can God Allow Evil?

You must be able to:

- Explain the problem of evil and suffering and how the problem may lead some people to reject belief in God or to question their faith
- Understand biblical teaching on suffering and the practical applications of Psalms, Job, prayer and charity.

Key Scripture and Religious Teaching

Genesis 2:16–17, 'And the LORD God commanded the man, "You are free to eat from any tree in the garden; but you must not eat from the tree of the knowledge of good and evil, for when you eat from it you will certainly die."'

Job 1:8, 'Have you considered my servant Job? There is no one on earth like him; he is blameless and upright, a man who fears God and shuns evil.'

What is Theodicy?

- How can an all-loving God exist when we see so much suffering around us every day?
- Every day the news features suffering from around the world.
- Famine, disease, war and acts of violence all bring suffering to individuals and communities.
- An omnibenevolent God brings good to the world and not evil, yet with suffering in the world we have 'the problem of evil'. This is theodicy.
- The Greek philosopher Epicurus simplified the existence of suffering in the world:
  - If an all-powerful and perfectly good God exists, then evil does not;
  - There is evil in the world;
  - So, an all-powerful and perfectly good God does not exist.

Key Point

All of humanity experiences evil in some shape or form, which raises questions about the existence of an all-loving God.

The 'Fall of Man'

- In Genesis 2, Adam and Eve live in the perfect Garden of Eden but are tempted and eat fruit from the tree of knowledge of good and evil.
- This is against the will of God and they commit the first recorded sin in the Bible.
- The eating of the fruit shows Adam and Eve's free will as they chose to disobey the will of God.
- Disobeying God and sinning is known as the 'fall of man' – a separation from God, which meant that man had brought suffering upon himself.

- God then punished both Adam and Eve by burdening Eve with pain during childbirth and Adam with the difficulty of farming barren land outside of the Garden of Eden.
- Another consequence of the fall is that death will enter the world and humans will no longer live forever.
- Christians believe that God does not cause the suffering that we see, but through our 'free will' we cause it ourselves.

The Book of Job

- Believed to be the first biblical book written, Job tells of Satan challenging God over the faithfulness of a man called Job.
- Satan argues that Job follows God because he has been blessed with a good life.
- God allows Satan to test Job and throughout the book Satan fills Job's life with despair and tragedy.
- However, despite this, Job continues to worship God, who then restores Job's life to fullness.
- Jews and Christians both argue that this shows that God is not the cause of suffering but is able to remove it when it is part of his sovereign plan.

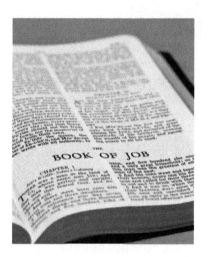

Role of Free Will in Religion

- A Muslim believes that all good comes from Allah, life on Earth is a test, and suffering in life is rewarded in the afterlife.
- Therefore, anyone who does not follow the will of Allah will face negative consequences when their life ends.
- Muslims also believe in the principle of free will.
- Muslims believe they were created with the wisdom to judge right from wrong and to make their own decisions. Many Muslims do, however, believe that Allah can intervene in their lives at any moment.
- Muslims believe that bad deeds lead people to learn not to repeat mistakes, as Allah allows people to make mistakes so that they can learn the right way and follow His teachings.
- Sikhs believe that humans suffer in this life as they either deny the existence of God, or act selfishly, not thinking of others.
- This suffering can be overcome by human effort, self-reflection, and divine grace (Gurprasad) through the Guru's teachings.
- Sikhs believe that evil itself or any demonic life forms do not exist.
- Instead they believe that only failings of the human spirit or conscience lead to actions that cause suffering to others.

Key Point

If God were to stop suffering from happening, it would deny humanity its free will.

Key Words

suffering
omnibenevolent
theodicy
free will
fall of man

Quick Test

1. How did Adam and Eve sin?
2. Why does God not stop us from sinning?
3. Why do people suffer according to Sikhs?

What Makes the Seven Sacraments Special?

You must be able to:

- Explore the nature of the seven sacraments in the Catholic Church
- Understand why they are important and how they are celebrated
- Investigate the specific sacraments of initiation.

Key Scripture and Religious Teaching

Luke 22:19, 'And he took bread, gave thanks and broke it, and gave it to them, saying, "This is my body given for you; do this in remembrance of me."'

What is a Sacrament?

- Catholics believe that a sacrament is a rite or ritual instituted by Jesus.
- It is a means of imparting God's grace and is a visible sign of that inward grace.
- Sacraments are signs of God's presence.

> **Key Point**
>
> A sacrament is a rite or ritual instituted by Jesus.

Initiation Sacraments (Baptism, Confirmation and Eucharist)

- Baptism is the first of the Catholic initiation sacraments.
- It involves pouring water onto the person's head while reciting the baptismal formula.
- Water is sometimes sprinkled, but this is not common.
- These words are said: 'I baptise you in the name of the Father, the Son and the Holy Spirit'.
- Baptism is symbolic of washing and of dying and rising with Christ.
- The sacrament of confirmation confirms and strengthens baptism. It is sometimes known as Chrismation.
- Confirmation is conducted by a bishop when the recipient is old enough to understand what they are doing.
- He places his hands on the person's head and says 'receive the Holy Spirit'.
- Each participant is anointed with oil.
- They renew their baptismal vows.
- For Catholics, the Eucharist 'completes Christian initiation'. It is also known as Holy Communion.
- Believers receive the 'body and blood of Christ' in bread and wine from a priest.
- Transubstantiation is the belief that the elements of the bread and wine change into the body and blood of Christ.

Healing Sacraments (Confession and Anointing the Sick)

- Confession is also known as the sacrament of penance.
- A baptised person can find spiritual healing.
- The person must show sincere remorse for their sin and be repentant.
- Confession must be made to a priest.
- The priest gives absolution (the taking away of sin) for what is confessed.
- Sanctification follows, which usually involves some form of penance (making amends for wrong done).
- The priest is bound by the 'seal of confession'.
- In the sacrament of the Anointing of the Sick, a priest will anoint the person who is ill using oil specially blessed for the purpose, while reciting a prayer of blessing.
- It is for believers who are 'experiencing the difficulties inherent in the condition of grave illness or old age'.
- When used for someone in immediate danger of death, the sacrament is known as Extreme Unction.

Sacraments of Service (Holy Orders and Marriage)

- In the sacrament of Holy Orders, a man is made a deacon, a priest or a bishop. It can only be carried out by a bishop.
- This does not happen all at once but by degrees.
- A deacon can baptise, preach, and administer the Eucharist.
- As well as undertaking the same sacraments as the deacon, a priest can also consecrate the bread and wine, give absolutions and anoint the sick.
- A bishop can confirm and ordain.
- The sacrament of marriage (or matrimony) contributes to the mission of the Church through the birth and upbringing of children.
- The sacrament confers on them the grace they need for marriage.
- It is celebrated in the presence of a priest.
- The bond between husband and wife is a symbol of the union of Christ (the bridegroom) and the Church (the bride).
- Marriage between baptised Catholics cannot be dissolved (divorce), although it can be annulled.

 Key Point

A sacrament is a means of imparting God's grace and is a visible sign of that inward grace.

Quick Test

1. Describe what happens in infant baptism and what it symbolises.
2. How does confirmation 'confirm and strengthen baptism'?
3. What do Catholics mean by 'transubstantiation'?
4. What does the Catholic Church teach about the sacrament of marriage?

 Key Words

sacrament
baptism
confirmation
confession
absolution
marriage

Can Prayer Really Make a Difference?

You must be able to:

- Explore the nature of prayer in different religions
- Understand why people pray
- Investigate what helps people to pray effectively.

Key Scripture and Religious Teaching

Ephesians 6:18, 'And pray in the Spirit on all occasions with all kinds of prayers and requests. With this in mind, be alert and always keep on praying for all the Lord's people (saints).'

Why Pray?

- Believers may pray in order to seek guidance from God. They may want to show gratitude for what He has done for them.
- Believers ask God to meet their needs and the needs of others.
- They may want to express how wonderful they believe Him to be.
- Saying sorry for misdeeds and asking for forgiveness is important.
- An individual speaks privately to God in personal prayer, whereas communal prayer involves a group of believers.
- Devotion is the term given to describe how a believer can show commitment to their faith and to their god.

The Nature of Christian Prayer

- When Christians pray, they acknowledge God's power and goodness, and their own neediness and dependence.
- Prayer is considered to be an essential part of public worship.
- Private prayer is also seen as being very important.
- Prayer is sometimes thought of as 'conversation' with God.
- The Lord's Prayer is considered to be the most important Christian prayer because it is believed to come directly from Jesus.
- The Apostles' Creed is another important Christian prayer.
- The purpose of prayer is not to change God's mind but to align the believer's will to His.
- The acronym ACTS can be helpful. It stands for:
  - Adoration: expressing how wonderful God is;
  - Confession: saying sorry and asking for forgiveness;
  - Thanksgiving: showing gratitude for what God has done;
  - Supplication: asking God to meet a need (including intercession).
- For Catholics, the rosary is a string of beads used as an aid to memory when saying the Rosary (a collection of prayers).
- The Hail Mary, or Ave Maria, is a traditional Catholic prayer based on the encounter between Angel Gabriel and the Virgin Mary. Catholics ask the Virgin Mary to pray to God on their behalf.
- Many Christians kneel or close their eyes when praying.
- Others pray with their faces uplifted and their hands open.

Key Point
Prayer helps a believer to feel closer to God.

Key Point
The purpose of prayer is to align the believer's will to God's, not to try to change His mind.

Key Point
When praying, sincerity is essential.

- Vocal prayers may be sung or spoken, and may involve responses from the congregation.
- Mental prayers are personal thoughts and sometimes involve meditation and contemplation.

Muslims at Prayer

- Many Muslims pray five times every day: at dawn, midday, late afternoon, sunset and late evening.
- The call to prayer signals that it is soon time to pray.
- Prayer is called Salah (or Salat).
- The rak'ah are ritual movements relating directly to the particular element of prayer being said.
- The imam leads the prayers in the mosque.
- Muslims remove their shoes, cover their heads and perform wudu (ritual washing) before entering to pray.
- They face qiblah – the direction of Mecca – denoted by a niche in the wall called the mihrab.
- Muslims use a prayer mat, facing Mecca, when not in the mosque.

Jewish Prayer

- Prayer is essential for a Jew and should be practised three times a day: morning, afternoon and evening.
- Jews may use both extemporary and set prayers.
- Thanksgiving, praise and petition are the main forms of prayer.
- Jews believe that prayer draws them closer to God and helps them to further understand and obey His will.
- The siddur is a prayer book, used for regular daily prayers.
- Some Jewish men will wear a tallit at certain times when they pray, covering their heads.
- The tallit has fringes and knots to recall the 613 laws of the Torah.
- At the Western Wall in Jerusalem, believers slip written prayers into the cracks between the stones.

Sikh Prayer

- Although Sikhs have set times for prayer in the morning and evening, they believe that everyday actions and service should be part of 'continuous' prayer.
- Perhaps the most important prayer is the Ardas. It is in three parts:
  - Part 1: meditation on the Almighty and contemplation of the Gurus;
  - Part 2: remembering the sacrifices of Sikhs throughout history;
  - Part 3: supplication and asking for forgiveness.
- The Ardas is always said before moving or opening the Guru Granth Sahib and is used during important occasions.

Key Words
The Lord's Prayer
intercession
rosary
Rosary
meditation
contemplation
Salah
rak'ah
wudu
siddur
tallit

 Quick Test

1. Why do believers pray?
2. What is the most important Christian prayer?
3. What is a siddur?
4. What physical activities may be associated with prayer?

Is it Possible to Find God in the Past?

You must be able to:

- Explore the purpose, history and nature of pilgrimage
- Investigate the places visited on pilgrimage
- Discover why pilgrimage is still important.

Key Scripture and Religious Teaching

Luke 2:41–42, 'Every year Jesus' parents went to Jerusalem for the Festival of the Passover. When he was twelve years old, they went up to the festival, according to the custom.'

Pilgrimage

- A **pilgrimage** is **not** a holiday.
- It is a journey with the purpose of honouring God.
- It may be a journey undertaken in penance for sin.
- Some places have a special historical importance for believers.
- The quest for healing is a frequent reason.
- Pilgrimage is a religious requirement in some faiths.
- It may be undertaken purely out of devotion.
- **Pilgrims** visit holy sites to become closer to God.
- Pilgrimage gives the believer time for meditation and contemplation and helps them to better understand their faith.

> **Key Point**
>
> The purpose of pilgrimage is **not** to go on holiday, but to strengthen faith.

Christian Pilgrimage

- Many Christians visit places in Israel that were important in Jesus' life.
- Bethlehem is a popular destination for pilgrims as the birthplace of Jesus. A key site is the Church of the Nativity (right).
- Nazareth was where the angel Gabriel appeared to the Virgin Mary and where she, Joseph and Jesus lived as a family. Pilgrims visit the Basilica of the Annunciation, which was established there.
- Jerusalem holds many sites important to pilgrims, associated with the life, death and resurrection of Jesus.
- The holiest site in Jerusalem is the Church of the Holy Sepulchre, which marks the site of Golgotha, where Jesus was crucified.
- There are many places of pilgrimage associated with visions of the Virgin Mary, including Lourdes in France, where the Virgin Mary is believed to have appeared to a young girl called Bernadette Soubirous.
- Between February 11 and July 16, 1858, Bernadette saw apparitions of Mary 18 times. She was told to go tell the village priest to build a chapel here.

- A pool formed, which became a sacred spring. Its waters are believed to bring healing and millions of believers seek help there every year. A statue of the Virgin Mary now stands in a religious grotto at the Lourdes shrine.
- There are many sites of pilgrimage based on relics of the saints, e.g millions of Catholics visit St Peter's Basilica in Rome, where the remains of St Peter are believed to be buried.
- Other sites of Christian pilgrimage include Taizé (France), Walsingham (England) and Knock (Ireland).

Muslim Pilgrimage

- At least once in their life, Muslims must undertake pilgrimage to Mecca. This is Hajj, one of the Five Pillars of Islam.
- There are various stages to the Hajj:
    - Ihram – when Muslims purify themselves through cleansing and the wearing of special garments.
    - Tawaf – circling the Ka'ba seven times.
    - Pilgrims then travel between Safa and Marwa seven times before going to Mina.
    - Following morning prayers in Mina, pilgrims spend the day in prayer on the plains of Arafat.
    - That night is spent in the region of Muzdalifah.
    - The next day, pilgrims 'stone the devil' at Mina.
    - In the following days, the Ka'ba is circled and, in Mina, the 'devil stoned' again.
    - The Hajj concludes by circling the Ka'ba again.

Jewish and Sikh Pilgrimage

- Jerusalem is the centre of faith for Jews.
- Adult male Jews used to be required to visit the Temple and offer sacrifices, especially during Passover.
- Today, the remaining wall of the Temple (the Western Wall, otherwise known as the Wailing Wall) is the most sacred site for devout Jews (right).
- Some boys have their Bar Mitzvah at the Wailing Wall and it is viewed as a special place to pray.
- Other sites that Jews visit include Masada, the Holocaust memorial (Yad Vashem) and Mount Sinai.
- The Sikh religion does not place great importance on pilgrimage but the Golden Temple, in Amritsar, India, is a sacred site for Sikhs.

Key Point

Believers want to tread in the footsteps of their important religious founders and leaders.

Quick Test

1. Why do people go on pilgrimage?
2. Why would pilgrims want to visit Israel?
3. Describe why Lourdes is important.
4. What is the Hajj?
5. What would Jews do at the Wailing Wall?

Key Words

pilgrimage
pilgrim
apparition
sacred
Hajj
Bar Mitzvah

Who is God?

1 What does the term 'Trinity' mean in Christianity? [2]

....

....

2 What does Genesis chapter 1 reveal about God the Father? [2]

....

....

3 Give three of the names given to God the Son. [2]

....

....

4 On what key scriptures do Christians base their beliefs around the Trinity? [4]

....

....

....

....

5 How does the Trinity help Christians to understand the true nature of God? [5]

....

....

....

....

....

Total Marks .... / 15

What Makes Jesus Special?

1 What set Jesus' birth apart from the birth of others? [2]

....

....

2 Who were the first people to hear of Jesus' birth? [2]

....

....

3 Briefly describe the key events just prior to the beginning of Jesus' three years of ministry. [2]

....

....

4 Explain how Jesus' death can be described as an act of redemption. [4]

....

....

....

....

5 What do you think is the significance of Jesus' death and resurrection for the Christian faith? [5]

....

....

....

....

....

Total Marks .... / 15

Practice Questions

Is Death a Comma or a Full Stop?

1. According to Christianity, where are humans to spend eternity following judgement? [2]

2. How is a Muslim prepared for burial? [2]

3. How is a Sikh body prepared prior to the funeral? [2]

4. Describe the belief of reincarnation in the Sikh faith. [4]

5. How can the Bible be used to argue for the existence of heaven and hell? [5]

Total Marks .... / 15

How Are We Judged After Death?

1 Where do the majority of Protestant Christians believe the soul will be sent after death? [1]

_____

_____

2 What does NDE mean and what are they? [2]

_____

_____

3 What is stated in John 3:16? [2]

_____

_____

4 What do Christians believe will happen in the afterlife? [4]

_____

_____

_____

_____

5 How does the Qur'an state that Muslims will be judged? [5]

_____

_____

_____

_____

_____

Total Marks _____ / 14

Practice Questions

How Can God Allow Evil?

1 What does the word 'theodicy' mean? [2]

_____

_____

2 How is the book of Job helpful for Christians who are struggling with the suffering in the world? [2]

_____

_____

3 What is 'free will'? [2]

_____

_____

4 Define the Sikh view of suffering and how it can be overcome. [4]

_____

_____

_____

_____

5 Explain how humankind lost its original relationship with God. [5]

_____

_____

_____

_____

_____

_____

Total Marks _____ / 15

What Makes the Seven Sacraments Special?

1 Which two sacraments mark age-related stages of life? [2]

....

....

2 Explain the purpose of confession. [2]

....

....

3 What are the similarities between confirmation and baptism? [2]

....

....

4 Why is Anointing of the Sick so important for Catholics? [4]

....

....

....

....

5 What makes marriage a sacrament? [5]

....

....

....

....

....

Total Marks .... / 15

Practice Questions

Can Prayer Really Make a Difference?

1. What is prayer? [2]

2. What can Catholics use to aid prayer and how do they help? [2]

3. What prayer is inspired by a key event in the life of Mary? [2]

4. How can the acronym ACTS help someone during a time of prayer? [4]

5. How can a Christian pray? [5]

Total Marks _____ / 15

Is it Possible to Find God in the Past?

1 Name two places of pilgrimage for Christians. [2]

2 Why do Christians visit Lourdes in France? [2]

3 How can pilgrimage be important to a believer? [2]

4 Define what a pilgrimage is. [4]

5 If a Christian wanted to feel closer to Jesus, where might they go on a pilgrimage and why? [5]

Total Marks _____ / 15

Does God Exist?

You must be able to:

- Describe beliefs and teachings about the nature and importance of God
- Explain the characteristics given to God, including omnipotence, omnibenevolence and omniscience
- Give examples of how these characteristics are shown in the Bible and personal experience.

> ### Key Scripture and Religious Teaching
>
> The Nicene Creed – This outlines the key beliefs of Christianity including beliefs in God.
>
> Genesis 1:1–2, 'In the beginning God created the heavens and the earth. Now the earth was formless and empty, darkness was over the surface of the deep, and the Spirit of God was hovering over the waters. And God said, "Let there be light," and there was light.'

Are You a Believer?

- It can be argued that, at some point, all humans consider their beliefs about the existence of a god.
- The majority of people in the world are either theist, believing in a specific god who governs the universe, or deist, believing in a disinterested deity with no personal relationship with the universe.
- They may believe in a single god, monotheist, or many gods, polytheist.
- Those who are as yet unsure of their beliefs are described as being agnostic, while those who have concluded that there is no divine being are atheist.

The Trinity

- Jesus the Christ (the Messiah), together with the Father and the Holy Spirit are known as the Trinity.
- Christians believe that there is one god who reveals Himself in three different expressions or persons.
- God is the Creator of all things that we see but still interacts personally with humanity.
- Jesus is a perfect revelation of God in human form and His death and resurrection have opened the way to forgiveness and eternal life.
- The Holy Spirit is the power of God on Earth and descended from heaven during Pentecost, following the ascension of Jesus.
- In the centuries following the life of Jesus, Christianity spread internationally until it became the official religion of the Roman Empire.

> ### Key Point
>
> The Christian God is one being with three different but simultaneous expressions.

The Characteristics of God

- God is described as having key characteristics that separate Him from the rest of His creation.
- Omnipotent – God is an all-powerful being, not subject to physical limitations, and is able to create and manipulate however He desires.
- Omniscient – God is all-knowing, aware of all actions and decisions that have ever taken place, are taking place and will ever take place in the future.
- Omnipresent – God is present in all places at all times, both in the physical and spiritual dimensions, with the exception of hell.
- Omnibenevolent – God is all good and all loving and is incapable of creating evil.
- Eternal – God was not created, having always been in existence and will always be in existence.

The Book of Revelation

- The book of Revelation appears at the end of the Bible and is different from all other books that come before it.
- Revelation recounts events and history, features poems and songs or addresses the early Church in the form of a letter.
- Revelation is an account of a series of dreams and visions revealed to John about the end of the world.
- The verses of the book recount the end times and describe events from the Rapture through to the end of the Earth.
- Many Christians point to events of the modern day world as illustration that the end is nigh, proving the existence of God.

Can God's Existence Be Proven?

- Many attempts have been made to prove that God exists.
- Many theological arguments have been written to show evidence both physically and spiritually as to how God exists.
- Thousands of books have been written accounting personal experiences with God, including references to miracles and visions.
- Many Christians believe that the simple answer is that God's existence will only be 'proven' on a personal level to the individual or if the verses of Revelation come to pass.

Quick Test

1. Describe the key characteristics of God.
2. What is the name given to the belief in many gods?
3. Explain the difference between a monotheistic and polytheistic religion.
4. Which category of belief do you think that you fall into?

Key Words

theist
monotheism
polytheism
agnostic
atheist

What Do They Believe?

You must be able to:

- Investigate Christian beliefs
- Examine what Muslims believe
- Explore what Jews believe
- Explore what Sikhs believe.

Christianity

Key Scripture and Religious Teaching

John 1:1–2, 'In the beginning was the Word, and the Word was with God, and the Word was God. He was with God in the beginning.'

- Christians believe that Jesus is the second 'person' of the Trinity and is God, together with the Father and the Holy Spirit.
- The Father created all things, Jesus is the Saviour and the Holy Spirit is the sustainer.
- Believers are equal, but some churches are led by priests, vicars and ministers.
- The Bible (holy book) contains the Old and New Testaments.
- The Old Testament relates the relationship between God and the people of Israel.
- The New Testament is about the birth, life, death and resurrection of Jesus and the subsequent spread of the Church.
- Christians try to follow the example and teaching of Jesus.
- Christians believe in life after death in either heaven or hell.

Key Point

The Bible contains the Old and New Testaments.

Islam

Key Scripture and Religious Teaching

'Ash-hadu an la ilaha illallah
Wa ash-hadu anna Muhammadan rasulullah'

'I bear witness that there is no God except Allah
And I bear witness that Muhammad is the messenger of Allah.'

The Shahadah

- Muslims believe there is only one God – Allah. Muhammad is the final and most important prophet in Islam, to whom the Qur'an was revealed.
- After death, Muslims believe that there is a day of judgement, with heaven for the faithful and hell for the unbeliever.
- The foundations of Islam are known as the Five Pillars.
- Submission to the will of Allah is the main goal for a Muslim.

Key Point

The Five Pillars of Islam are the foundation of a Muslim's everyday life.

Judaism

Key Scripture and Religious Teaching

'Sh'ma Yisra'eil Adonai Eloheinu Adonai echad.'

'Hear, O Israel, the Lord is our God, the Lord is One.' (Deuteronomy 6:4–9)

- The Torah is the most important of the Hebrew texts, containing the Law of Moses. Other Jewish scripture, the Tenakh, contains books of prophecy, poetry, history, a moral code and spiritual guidance.
- Yahweh is the holiest name that Jews give to God. In the Torah, the vowels of Yahweh were removed so it could not be spoken.
- Jews believe Yahweh to be the one God: all-powerful and all-knowing. Genesis describes Him as the Creator of all things.
- Abraham is considered to be the father of the Hebrew nation and Moses the founder of the faith.
- Jews live in 'covenant' with God and obey the 'mitzvot' (commandments).
- Some Jews believe that there will be a judgement (perhaps after the arrival of the Messiah) resulting in a place in 'heaven' or 'hell'.
- Other Jews believe that judgement is here and now.
- Unlike Christians, Jews are still awaiting the coming of the 'Messiah'.

Sikhism

Key Scripture and Religious Teaching

The Guru Granth Sahib begins with the Mool Mantar (also sometimes spelled Mool Mantra):
'Ik ōaṅgkār sat nām kartā purkh nirbha'u nirvair akāl mūrat ajūnī saibhaṅ gur prasād.'

'The One of which everything is and continuous, the ever existing, creator being personified, without fear, without hatred, image of the timeless being, beyond birth, self-existent, by Guru's Grace.'

- The Sikh holy book is the Guru Granth Sahib.
- The Mool Mantar means 'basic teaching' of Sikhism.
- Sikhs believe that there is only one God; without form or gender.
- There are no priests or ministers in Sikhism because all are equal and all have equal access to God.
- Doing good deeds for others is important, as is meditating on God.
- The cycle of birth, life, death and rebirth is a key part of Sikh faith.
- The behaviour of a person in their previous life dictates the quality of this existence, known as the Law of Karma.

Key Words

Trinity
Bible
Qur'an
Five Pillars
Torah
Guru Granth Sahib
Mool Mantar

Quick Test

1. What is the New Testament about?
2. What is the main goal for Muslims?

How Do They Worship?

You must be able to:

- Investigate how Christians worship
- Examine how Muslims worship
- Explore how Jews worship
- Explore how Sikhs worship.

Key Scripture and Religious Teaching

Acts 2:42, 'They devoted themselves to the apostles' teaching and to fellowship, to the breaking of bread and to prayer.'

Christianity

- Christians can worship at home, but more usually at church.
- Worship usually takes place on Sunday for about 1–1.5 hours.
- In some denominations, anyone can lead worship; however, it is often led by a minister, vicar or priest.
- Services may contain readings from the Bible, hymns and songs, prayers and a sermon.
- During Holy Communion, bread and wine represent the body and blood of Jesus.
- The cross, altar, font and pulpit are often key features in a church.
- Men, women and children can sit together in worship.

Islam

- Muslims hold their main collective worship on Friday in a mosque.
- Worship at home and in the mosque is dominated by prayer.
- The call to prayer is issued five times a day from the minaret, by the muezzin.
- Muslims must remove their shoes and carry out ritual washing, called wudu, before entering the mosque.
- They sit on the floor of the prayer hall facing the direction of Mecca (indicated by a niche in the wall called the mihrab). Women sit separately to men.
- Muslims may pray in a clean, appropriate place on a prayer mat facing Mecca if they cannot attend a mosque.
- The ritual prayer, Salah or Salat, is one of the Five Pillars of Islam and occurs at dawn, midday, late afternoon, sunset and between sunset and midnight.
- Although prayers occur in the mosque throughout the week, Friday prayer (the Jumu'ah) is the most important. It is led by an imam and occurs just after noon.
- The Qur'an is read, a sermon preached and the ritual prayers undertaken.

Key Point

Christian worship usually occurs in a church on Sunday.

Key Point

Prayer is central to the Muslim faith, both in the home and in the mosque.

Judaism

- Jews meet for collective worship in a synagogue on the Sabbath (Friday evening until Saturday evening).
- Worship is led by a rabbi and the service conducted in Hebrew.
- There are no musical instruments in Jewish worship; singing is led by a cantor (song leader).
- Reading from scripture is the central part of the service.
- The Torah can only be taken out of the Ark (where the scrolls are kept) and read in worship when there is a minyan (a minimum of ten adult male Jews) present.
- Everyone stands when the Torah is taken to the bimah.
- Readings from the scriptures, prayers, singing psalms and a sermon usually make up the main elements of worship.
- Men and women are separated, in Orthodox synagogues, by a screen or a balcony.
- As a sign of respect, hats are commonly worn by men in worship. Men usually wear a yarmulke (a small round cap) and a tallit (prayer shawl).
- Many elements of Jewish worship are based in the home.

Sikhism

- Sikhs can worship in private or publicly together (sangat) in a Gurdwara (right). There is no specific holy day for Sikhs but most services in England are on Sunday.
- Any Sikh, male or female, can lead worship in a Gurdwara.
- The Granthi is a Sikh who has been trained to read the scriptures and organise worship.
- In the Gurdwara, Sikhs bow before the Guru Granth Sahib, which is placed on the takht (raised platform).
- The Granthi will wave a chauri (fan) over the book.
- Food and money are placed before the Guru Granth Sahib.
- Men and women sit separately.
- Services contain readings from the Guru Granth Sahib, hymns (accompanied by musical instruments), prayers and a sermon.
- Kara Parshad (sacred food) is shared by all at the end of the service.
- After the service, everyone goes to the langar hall (communal kitchen), where they share a meal.
- Gurpurbs are festivals that are associated with the lives of the Gurus and are usually celebrated with an Akhand Path.

Key Point

The home and the synagogue are central to the Jewish faith.

Key Point

Sikh faith is centred in and around the Gurdwara.

Key Words

pulpit
font
wudu
synagogue
bimah
Gurdwara
Granthi
Kara Parshad
Gurpurbs

Quick Test

1. Who can lead Christian worship?
2. When does the Jumu'ah occur and who leads it?
3. Outline what usually happens during worship in a synagogue.

What Makes Christian Worship Different?

You must be able to:

- Investigate why Christians worship
- Explore what happens when Christians worship
- Consider the different styles of worship.

Key Scripture and Religious Teaching

Acts 2:46, 'Every day they continued to meet together in the temple courts. They broke bread in their homes and ate together with glad and sincere hearts.'

Origins

- The origins of Christian worship can be found in synagogue worship. Jesus and His followers celebrated the important Jewish festivals. They regularly attended synagogue on Saturdays.
- Christians worship, however, on Sundays. Sunday became important because of Easter Day – the day Christians believe Jesus was raised back to life.
- Early Christians met in private houses; more and more special church buildings for public worship were constructed later.

Purpose

- Although Christians can worship at home, they usually worship in a church.
- Worshipping together helps believers encourage each other in their faith.
- Christians worship together because Jesus promised to be with them when they did so.
- They also believe that the Holy Spirit is present to help guide their worship and lead them to a deeper relationship with God.

Elements

- Christian worship may contain various elements to help worshippers praise God and communicate with Him.
- Music, in the form of hymns and songs, enables worshippers to enter into the presence of God.
- Instrumental music is often used to aid prayer and meditation.
- Worship contains different types of prayer to give an opportunity for Christians to talk and listen to God.
- Prayers may be pre-written and read out loud or extempore (made up in the moment).

- Readings from the Bible play a crucial part in worship, helping Christians to hear the 'word of God'.
- There is usually a sermon (a religious talk), which explains something about the Bible or about Christian living.
- There may often be a section of the service where bread and wine are consumed (Holy Communion/Eucharist).
- Some churches may include drama, mime, dance or video in order to help communicate something of the message.
- Many churches now use modern instruments and music styles in their worship, rather than an organ and traditional hymns.
- Worship usually lasts for about 1–1.5 hours.

> **Key Point**
>
> Different types of prayer are central to most worship services.

Style

- Styles of worship can vary greatly.
- Some churches have intricate worship with rich and complex ritual.
- Others have very simple worship with little ritual.
- In other worship, reading and explaining the Bible takes priority.
- In some services, Holy Communion is most important, during which bread and wine represent the body and blood of Jesus.
- In some denominations, anyone can lead worship; however, it is often led by a minister, vicar or priest.
- The cross, altar, font and pulpit are important features in some churches.
- Men, women and children can sit together in worship.

Festivals

- Festivals are important in Christian worship and recall important events in the life of Jesus or the early Church.
- Christmas recalls the birth of Jesus.
- Special services are held that include readings and carols about the birth of Jesus.
- Some churches have nativity plays, often performed by children.
- Easter remembers the death and resurrection of Jesus.
- Solemn Good Friday services give way to joyful worship on Easter Sunday.
- Pentecost celebrates the gift of the Holy Spirit to the disciples and reminds Christians that God's power can help them.

> **Quick Test**
>
> 1. Why do Christians worship?
> 2. When do Christians worship?
> 3. Where do Christians worship?
> 4. Why is Easter important?

> **Key Words**
>
> sermon
> Holy Communion
> Easter
> Pentecost

How Does Scripture Guide Christian Life?

You must be able to:

- Explore the nature of the Bible
- Discover why it is important to believers
- Investigate the content of the Old and New Testament.

Key Scripture and Religious Teaching

Psalm 19:7-8,
'The law of the LORD is perfect, refreshing the soul.
The statutes of the LORD are trustworthy, making wise the simple.
The precepts of the LORD are right, giving joy to the heart.
The commands of the LORD are radiant, giving light to the eyes.'

The Bible

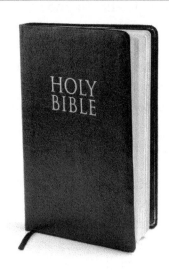

- The Bible is a library of books.
- It was written by many different men over many centuries.
- There are 66 books, contained in two separate collections.
- Collection one is known as the Old Testament.
- The Old Testament is about the relationship between Yahweh (the Hebrew name for God) and the people of Israel.
- Collection two is the New Testament.
- It deals with the coming of Jesus, the Messiah (Christ).
- The New Testament also explores how His followers continued His ministry after His death and resurrection.
- Bibles are treated with great respect.
- Believers feel that God 'speaks' to them through the Bible.
- Reading from the Bible takes place in collective worship.
- Believers read the scriptures as part of their private devotions, to learn about God and His relationship with His people.
- Christians try to live according to the Bible's moral teaching.
- The Bible offers spiritual guidance to believers.

> ### Key Point
>
> Christians believe that the Bible is the 'inspired Word of God'.

The Old Testament

- Originally written in Hebrew, the Old Testament contains 39 books.
- The first five books are often known as the Books of Moses or the Pentateuch.
- They deal with creation through to the Exodus and giving of the Law.

- There are historical books dealing with the foundation of the nation and the establishment of the monarchy.
- Books such as Judges, 1 and 2 Samuel and 1 and 2 Kings outline the establishment of the nation.
- Books such as Job, Psalms and Proverbs are poetic books and are often used for personal devotion.
- The Books of the Prophets (Amos, Hosea, Isaiah, Jeremiah, Ezekiel and others) deal with Yahweh's relationship with His people.
- These individuals were used by God to guide His people through difficult times.

The New Testament

- Originally written in Greek, the New Testament records the coming of Jesus and its impact.
- The four Gospels recount the birth, life, ministry, death and resurrection of Jesus.
- Only Matthew and Luke relate the events surrounding Jesus' birth.
- Matthew, Mark and Luke are often referred to as the Synoptic Gospels because of their similarity.
- The word 'synoptic' is Greek and means 'seen together'.
- They follow the same basic chronology, although they each have their own influences and sources.
- The Gospel of John is very different; it does not follow the same chronology as the others and appears to be more theological.
- John's treatment of the miracles and teaching of Jesus is also very different.
- The Acts of the Apostles tells the story of how the disciples spread the Kingdom of God, starting from Jerusalem and then out into the Gentile world.
- It was written by Luke (also the author of the Gospel).
- The main characters are Peter, who was the foundation of the early Church, and Paul, missionary to the Gentiles.
- There is also a collection of letters, or epistles.
- Most of them were written by Paul to churches and individuals in the early years.
- Other letters were written by people such as Peter, James and John.
- The final book (the book of Revelation) contains spiritual and moral guidance, prophecy and mystical teaching and is credited to the apostle John.

 Key Point

Christians try to live according to the Bible's moral teaching.

> **Quick Test**

1. Why is the Bible sometimes called 'a library' of books?
2. Outline why the Bible is important to Christians.
3. What are the main types of literature in the Old Testament?
4. How is John's Gospel different from the other three?

Key Words

Testament
Messiah
Pentateuch
Gospel
synoptic
epistle

Other Scriptures

You must be able to:

- Examine the Muslim scriptures
- Explore the Jewish scriptures
- Investigate the Sikh scriptures.

The Qur'an

- The angel Gabriel (Jibril) appeared to Muhammad and revealed the will of Allah to him. Muhammad 'recited' these words until he had learned them by heart.
- The Qur'an contains the 'recitations' (Qur'an is Arabic and means 'he recited').
- Muhammad collected disciples and relayed these teachings to them.
- After his death, the first Caliph, Abu Bakr, encouraged his followers to collect his teachings together in what is now known as the Qur'an.
- Despite the Qur'an being translated into many languages, Muslims still learn to read and recite it in the original Arabic.
- The Qur'an is composed of 114 chapters (or surahs).
- Muslims believe the Qur'an to be the inspired word of Allah and treat it with the greatest respect.
- A Muslim who memorises the Qur'an is known as a 'hafiz'.

Key Point

All Muslims learn Arabic so that they can read the Qur'an in its original language.

The Tenakh

- The Tenakh contains 39 books.
- The Tenakh contains the Torah ('Teaching'), the Nevi'im ('Prophets') and the Ketuvim ('Writings').
- The five books of the Torah are the most important and are often known as the Books of Moses or the Pentateuch.
- Books such as Judges, 1 and 2 Samuel, and 1 and 2 Kings, are historical books and outline the foundation of the nation and the establishment of the monarchy.
- Books such as Job, Psalms and Proverbs are poetic books and are often used for personal devotion by both Jews and Christians.
- The Books of the Prophets are about Yahweh's relationship with His people.
- Through various people (Amos, Hosea, Isaiah, Jeremiah, Ezekiel and others) God guided and challenged the people of Israel to be faithful and, later, be restored to their homeland.
- The Torah scrolls are handwritten in Hebrew. They are extremely expensive to produce.

Key Point

The Talmud is the written version of Jewish oral law.

- Each section is written on parchment and then glued onto the scroll.
- If a mistake is made, the whole section has to be re-written.
- When being read, the text is never touched by hand.
- A yad (metal pointer) is used to follow the reading.
- At the end of its life, a scroll is not destroyed but given a ceremonial burial.

Guru Granth Sahib

- The Guru Granth Sahib (the Living Guru) is a collection of teachings and hymns written by a variety of Sikh Gurus over many years.
- Guru Nanak (1469–1539) was the founder of Sikhism and the first of the ten Sikh Gurus.
- Guru Nanak's hymns and teachings were written down and contributions added to the scriptures by other Gurus.
- Eventually the tenth Guru, Guru Gobind Singh, decreed that after his death there should be no more human Gurus: the Guru Granth Sahib should take their place.
- All copies of the Guru Granth Sahib are identical in layout.
- There are 1430 pages and every verse is in the same place on the same page.
- Respect for the Guru Granth Sahib is shown in different ways:
  – Bathing before handling it;
  – Keeping it in its own room when not in use;
  – Carrying it above the head when moving it;
  – Important decisions are made only after reading it;
  – Sikhs must remove their shoes and cover their heads before coming into the presence of the book.
- Akhand Path is the continuous recitation (without any break) of the Guru Granth Sahib from beginning to end, lasting about 48 hours, by a team of readers.

Key Point
The Guru Granth Sahib is the final Guru.

Points to Consider

- Consider:
  – why each faith believe their scriptures to be so important;
  – whether **all** of the different scriptures can be 'true';
  – the statement, 'Holy books are the words of men and not of God'.

 Quick Test

1. Describe the compilation of the Qur'an.
2. How did the Qur'an come into existence?
3. What is the difference between the Tenakh and the Talmud?
4. Explain how the Guru Granth Sahib was composed and what it contains.
5. How do Sikhs show respect to the Guru Granth Sahib?

 Key Words

Qur'an
Tenakh
Torah
Guru Granth Sahib

How Do They Live Their Lives?

You must be able to:

- Consider the effect of faith on a Christian's life
- Explore how faith affects a Muslim's way of life
- Investigate the relevance of faith for Jewish living
- Consider the effect of faith on a Sikh's life.

Christianity

- Some Christians will wear a cross or crucifix to remind them of the death and resurrection of Jesus.
- Christians may spend time each day reading the Bible and praying.
- Rosary beads (right) are used by Catholics to help with prayer.
- Christians may meet together in small groups for fellowship.
- Rites of passage are important for Christians with birth (baptism/dedication), adolescence (confirmation/adult baptism), marriage (wedding) and death (funeral) being marked with special services.
- Evangelical Christians actively try to persuade others to become Christians.
- Some Christians study for years to become priests, vicars or ministers.
- Nuns and monks are Christians who have withdrawn from everyday life to concentrate on prayer or serving the poor.
- Lots of Christians regularly spend their free time practically serving the poor and homeless.

Key Point
Christians often read the Bible and pray at home.

Islam

- A Muslim's daily life is governed by the Five Pillars:
  - The Shahadah is the profession of faith: 'there is no God but Allah and Muhammad is His prophet (messenger)'. When a Muslim recites this, they personally accept it as true and that they will obey all the commitments of Islam in their life. It is the first of the Five Pillars of Islam.
  - Salah is the ritual prayers that are offered five times a day in response to the call to prayer by the muezzin.
  - Zakah is the systematic collection of 2.5% of a Muslim's wealth, which is given to the poor.
  - Sawm is when Muslims are required to fast during daylight hours throughout the month of Ramadan. It ends with the festival of Eid-ul-Fitr.
  - Hajj: at least once in their lives, Muslims are expected to go on pilgrimage to Mecca (right).
- Halal (Arabic for 'permissible') food is that which adheres to Islamic law, as defined in the Qur'an. The criteria specify what foods are allowed and how the food must be prepared.
- For example, animals must be alive and healthy at the time of slaughter and all blood is drained from the carcass.

Judaism

- The synagogue is not just the place of Jewish worship but is also a centre for community and education. The Ark (where the scrolls are kept), the bimah (reading desk) and the ner tamid (eternal light) are among the main features.
- Food laws strictly govern what Jews can eat. There are detailed teachings on what cannot be eaten and what is kosher.
- Rites of passage (such as Brit Milah, Bar and Bat Mitzvah) are significant times in a Jew's life. There are also special ceremonies for marriage and death.
- Shabbat (the Sabbath) is observed both at home and in the synagogue, beginning at sunset on Friday and ending at sunset on Saturday. It is a day set aside for rest and worship and there are strict rules about what work can be done during this time.
- There are many Jews who would not closely observe kosher or the Sabbath. They may class themselves as 'Reform Jews', with more traditional believers often described as 'Orthodox'.
- Festivals are very important in Jewish life, including Rosh Hashanah (New Year), Yom Kippur (Day of Atonement), Pesach (Passover), Shavuot (Feast of Weeks), Sukkott (Feast of Booths) and Hanukkah. They are often celebrated in the home and frequently have a historical significance.

Sikhism

- A Sikh may wake early, bathe and begin the day by meditating on God.
- There are set prayers that a Sikh should recite in the morning (including the Mool Mantar), the evening and before going to sleep.
- In 1699, Guru Gobind Singh formed the Khalsa and introduced the Five Ks.
- The wearing of the Five Ks is a daily public demonstration of a Sikh's worship and devotion. They are:
  - Kesh (uncut hair) – holiness and strength;
  - Kara (a steel bracelet) – restraint and gentleness;
  - Kanga (a wooden comb) – clean mind and clean body;
  - Kaccha (cotton underwear) – chastity;
  - Kirpan (steel sword) – struggle against injustice.
- Sikhism requires service to Waheguru (God), to the Khalsa and to all of humanity.
- An important aspect of Sikhism is to provide a service to the community (Sewa).

Key Point

Religious symbols are key to a Sikh's faith.

Key Words

crucifix
fellowship
Shahadah
Zakah
sawm
Hajj
kosher
Shabbat
Yom Kippur
Khalsa

Quick Test

1. Why is the cross important for Christians?
2. Why is pilgrimage to Mecca important to Muslims?
3. Why are dietary laws important for Jews?
4. What are the Five Ks?

Review Questions

Who is God?

1 Name one member of the Trinity. [1]

2 What does the characteristic of 'omnipotent' mean when referring to God? [1]

3 In Genesis 1, who created the universe? [1]

4 Explain the importance of God being omnibenevolent. [4]

5 'God cannot exist, as the presence of the Holy Spirit on Earth would see all people believing in His existence.'

Explain three reasons why some may agree with this statement and three reasons why others may disagree with this statement. [6]

Total Marks _____ / 13

What Makes Jesus Special?

1 How is Jesus referred to in John 1:1? [1]

2 Name one of the Gospels that records the miraculous virgin birth of Jesus. [1]

3 Which ruler wanted to see Jesus dead soon after His birth? [1]

4 How do you think Christians can lead a moral life by following the teachings of Jesus? [3]

5 'Jesus' death and resurrection should lead Christians to focus on the afterlife as opposed to this life.'

Explain three reasons why some may agree with this statement and three reasons why others may disagree with this statement. [6]

Total Marks .... / 12

Is Death a Comma or a Full Stop?

1 What is the name given to rebirth in Sikhism? [1]

2 When someone dies, what rite of passage takes place? [1]

3 In Catholicism, where might a soul be sent after death if it is not ready for heaven? [1]

4 Explain the principle of karma in Sikhism. [4]

5 'With the world growing at an ever-faster rate, all humans should be cremated after death to conserve resources and space.'

Explain three reasons why some may agree with this statement and three reasons why others may disagree with this statement. [6]

Total Marks _____ / 13

How Are We Judged After Death?

1 What biblical rules guide both Jews and Christians alike? [1]

2 Where do Christians believe Jesus ascended to? [1]

3 What is the sixth of the Ten Commandments? [1]

4 Explain the Christian view of how hell came into existence. [4]

5 'It is wrong to live this life always thinking about what might happen when we die.'

Explain three reasons why some may agree with this statement and three reasons why others may disagree with this statement. [6]

Total Marks _____ / 13

Review Questions

How Can God Allow Evil?

1. What is the term given to 'the problem of evil'? [1]

2. Define the term 'sin'. [1]

3. How might a Christian define suffering? [1]

4. Describe the story of the first sin as told in Genesis 2. [4]

5. 'The presence of so much evil in the world proves that an all-loving God cannot exist.'

   Explain three reasons why some may agree with this statement and three reasons why others may disagree with this statement. [6]

   Total Marks _____ / 13

What Makes the Seven Sacraments Special?

1 Which sacrament marks birth? [1]

2 Which sacrament do some Christians only take when they have completed the rite of confirmation? [1]

3 How can a Catholic say sorry for their sins after confession? [1]

4 Describe the nature of the Eucharist. [4]

5 Explain the role and purpose of confession in the Catholic Church. [6]

Total Marks _____ / 13

Review Questions

Can Prayer Really Make a Difference?

1 Name a key Catholic prayer. [1]

2 What is the main purpose of devotion? [1]

3 What is the name given to prayer when two or more people pray together? [1]

4 Explain the importance of prayer in Christian life. [4]

5 'Praying for something to happen is not as important as acting to make something happen.'

Explain three reasons why some may agree with this statement and three reasons why others may disagree with this statement. [6]

Total Marks _____ / 13

Is it Possible to Find God in the Past?

1 Define what a pilgrimage is. [1]

2 Name a place a Christian may visit to feel closer to Jesus. [1]

3 Who is there a statue of in the grotto at Lourdes? [1]

4 How is Lourdes significant in Christian pilgrimage? [4]

5 'The cost of pilgrimage would be better used to help the poor.'

Explain three reasons why some may agree with this statement and three reasons why others may disagree with this statement. [6]

Total Marks _____ / 13

Practice Questions

Does God Exist?

1 What is the Nicene Creed? [2]

2 What part does the Holy Spirit play in the Trinity? [2]

3 What evidence is there for God's existence? [2]

4 Which four terms are used to describe the varying beliefs individuals hold in relation to the existence of God? Explain them. [4]

5 What are the key characteristics given to the Christian God? [5]

Total Marks _____ / 15

What Do They Believe?

1 What separates belief and fact? [2]

_____

_____

2 What are the key beliefs stated in the Shahadah? [2]

_____

_____

3 Give two Sikh beliefs about God. [2]

_____

_____

4 How does belief influence the life of a believer? [4]

_____

_____

_____

_____

5 What do Jews believe about God and their relationship with Him? [5]

_____

_____

_____

_____

_____

Total Marks _____ / 15

Practice Questions

How Do They Worship?

1 How would you define 'worship'?   [2]

_____

_____

2 What role can food play in worship?   [2]

_____

_____

3 How is Jewish worship led in the synagogue?   [2]

_____

_____

4 What are the main elements of a time of worship?   [4]

_____

_____

_____

_____

5 Describe the ritual of worship for a Muslim man when he visits a mosque.   [5]

_____

_____

_____

_____

_____

Total Marks _____ / 15

What Makes Christian Worship Different?

1 How can music help during worship? [2]

....

....

2 Why do Christians share bread and wine? [2]

....

....

3 Why is Pentecost important to Christians? [2]

....

....

4 Why do Christians worship? [4]

....

....

....

....

5 Describe the importance of festivals to Christians. [5]

....

....

....

....

....

Total Marks .... / 15

How Does Scripture Guide Christian Life?

1 Why do Christians believe that the Bible has authority? [2]

2 What are the two main sections of the Bible? [2]

3 What are the main two languages that the Bible was written in? [2]

4 Name the different types of writing found in the Old Testament. [4]

5 How is the Bible central to Christian life? [5]

Total Marks .... / 15

Other Scriptures

1 Who was the first writer of the Guru Granth Sahib and how many writers were there after him? [2]

2 Define the 'Akhand Path'. [2]

3 What two languages were the Qur'an and Torah originally written in? [2]

4 What are the three key sections of the Tenakh and how many books does it contain? [4]

5 Why do believers read their holy scriptures? [5]

Total Marks _____ / 15

How Do They Live Their Lives?

1 What is the Jewish holy day called and when does it take place? [2]

_____

_____

2 Name two festivals that a Jew will observe. [2]

_____

_____

3 What are the significant rites of passage in Jewish life? [2]

_____

_____

4 What does the Sabbath celebrate? [2]

_____

_____

5 Why do you think the rite of baptising babies was introduced? [3]

_____

_____

_____

6 What are the four rites of passage in Christianity?   [4]

....

....

....

....

7 What are the Five Pillars of Islam and how do they guide a Muslim's life?   [5]

....

....

....

....

....

Total Marks .... / 20

Jesus' Teaching

You must be able to:

- Explore the main teaching themes in Mark's Gospel
- Understand the purpose and meaning of parables
- Discover the importance of Jesus' teaching on discipleship.

> **Key Scripture and Religious Teaching**
>
> Mark 4:11–12, 'He told them, "The secret of the kingdom of God has been given to you.
> But to those on the outside everything is said in parables so that,
> 'they may be ever seeing but never perceiving,
> and ever hearing but never understanding;
> otherwise they might turn and be forgiven!'"

Main Teaching Themes in Mark

- There are a number of key themes in Mark's Gospel, including:
  - the Kingdom of God;
  - the nature and cost of discipleship;
  - the titles of Jesus;
  - the 'Messianic Secret'.

The Kingdom of God

- Jesus often delivered His teaching directly, such as His teaching about the Sabbath (Mark 2:23–28). However, He frequently taught the people in parables.
- A parable is a story with a hidden meaning.
- The parables became the hallmark of Jesus' teaching.
- Many of the parables in Mark's Gospel are about the Kingdom of God. These include:
  - the Sower (4:1–20);
  - the Lamp (4:21–25);
  - the Growing Seed (4:26–29);
  - the Mustard Seed (4:30–34).
- In these parables, Jesus teaches about how different things are in the coming Kingdom.
- He describes how the Kingdom will be and the role of believers.

> **Key Point**
>
> Jesus often taught in parables about the Kingdom of God.

Discipleship

- In Mark 8:34–36, Jesus explains that discipleship requires sacrifice.
- 'Taking up the cross' was a reality for Mark's readers in Rome, who faced persecution and death for their faith.

- In Mark 1:16–20, the call of the first disciples (Simon, Andrew, James and John) sees them leave their fishing nets and follow Him ('Come with me and I will make you fishers of men').
- Jesus explained that only those who were prepared to lose their life for Him and for the Gospel would save it.
- When Jesus sent out the 12 disciples in pairs, He commanded that they should take nothing with them and have absolute trust in God's provision (Mark 6:7–13).
- Disciples must be humble (Mark 9:35).
- In Mark 10:14–15, Jesus makes it clear that His followers must have a child-like faith (not child*ish*).
- Wealth can be a problem for disciples, as seen in the story of Jesus' encounter with the rich young man (Mark 10:17–31) and the reference to the camel and the eye of a needle. Some have suggested that this means that Jesus' disciples must sell their possessions to give to the poor.
- The discussion with James and John about sitting either side of Jesus reveals that anyone who wants to be great must be the servant of all (Mark 10:43–44).

The Titles of Jesus

- Various titles are linked with Jesus but three are prominent.
- Jesus is first referred to as the 'Messiah' (the Christ) in Mark chapter 1. The term 'Messiah' in the Old Testament described prophets, priests and kings.
- The title 'Son of God' is also found in Mark chapter 1. God himself uses the title at the baptism and the Transfiguration.
- The title 'Son of Man' can be found in the Old Testament books of Ezekiel and Daniel. It suggests kingship and glory.
- In Mark 14:62, Jesus applies the title 'Son of Man' to Himself and appears to relate it to His second coming. The title particularly highlights the humanity and humility of Jesus.

The 'Messianic Secret'

- The 'Messianic Secret' in Mark's Gospel was suggested by William Wrede to explain why Jesus wasn't more widely recognised as the Messiah during his ministry.
- Mark frequently records Jesus instructing demons (that He has driven out) and His disciples not to tell anyone about His Messiahship. Mark 8:29–30 is a good example, when Peter recognises Him as the Messiah and is forbidden to tell anyone.

Ministry of Jesus

You must be able to:

- Explore the nature and content of Mark's Gospel
- Investigate the key events in the life of Jesus.

Key Scripture and Religious Teaching

Mark 1:1, 'The beginning of the gospel about Jesus Christ, the Son of God'.

About Mark's Gospel

- Mark is considered to have been the earliest written of the Gospels (probably around 65AD).
- The author may have been the eyewitness almost arrested after the Last Supper in the Upper Room.
- Mark's Gospel is the shortest and gives a sense of urgency.
- There are no birth stories and the resurrection accounts are shorter than in the other Gospels.
- The ending is abrupt. Some believe the original ending was lost.

> **Key Point**
>
> The Gospel's author may have been the young man who was almost arrested after the Last Supper.

Early Days (Mark 1:1–20)

- The Gospel opens with Jesus being named as the Messiah and Son of God.
- As He is baptised by John, the Holy Spirit descends on Him like a dove and a heavenly voice announces Him as the Son of God.
- Jesus is tempted in the wilderness by Satan.
- Jesus begins to preach the Good News.
- Jesus calls His disciples and begins His public ministry.

Who Were the 12 Disciples?

- Jesus called 12 men to be His disciples and, later, apostles (Mark 3:13–19). They were recruited from different parts of the community Jesus grew up in.
- Jesus needed people He could trust to spread His teachings and the Christian religion after His death.
- Simon, also called Peter (the Rock), was a fisherman who became the leader of the Church after Jesus' death and resurrection; tradition has it that he was crucified upside down.
- Andrew was the brother of Simon and also a fisherman; he is believed to have taken the Gospel to Asia Minor.

- James (and John, his brother) were given the surname 'Boanerges' (sons of thunder); James is believed to have died a martyr at the hands of King Herod.
- John (Boanerges) was also one of the 'inner circle' of disciples and, like his brother, was a fisherman. He is sometimes known as 'John the Beloved' and later in life he was banished to the island of Patmos where he wrote the book of Revelation and the Gospel of John.
- Little is known of Philip but he came from Bethsaida (the same town as Andrew and Peter) and he was a Greek-speaker.
- Bartholomew (also known as Nathanael) was a friend of Philip, came from Cana in Galilee and is reported to have been martyred.
- Thomas (Didymus – 'a twin') is also known as 'Doubting Thomas' because he originally doubted Jesus' resurrection. Tradition states that Thomas was a missionary to India where he was martyred.
- Matthew (also known as Levi) was a tax collector. Some believe he authored Matthew's Gospel and that he died a martyr's death.
- Little is known about James, son of Alphaeus.
- Thaddaeus was also known as Judas and was James's brother.
- Simon 'the Zealot' was part of a Jewish resistance movement against Roman authority.
- Judas Iscariot was from a place called Kerioth and was in charge of the finances for the disciples. He betrayed Jesus for 30 pieces of silver and, later, committed suicide.

Key Point

Jesus had 12 disciples.

Key Events

- At Caesarea Philippi (right), Jesus asks the disciples who people say He is, with a variety of responses. When He asks them, 'but you, who do you say I am?', Peter answers that He is the Christ.
- Jesus commands him to silence and explains that the Son of Man must go to Jerusalem and be killed, but will rise again.
- At the Transfiguration, Jesus takes Peter, James and John away, and Moses and Elijah appear with Him. God tells the disciples, 'This is my son', but they do not understand.
- There were various conflicts with the Pharisees and Sadducees.
- Jesus rode into Jerusalem where He was hailed as one who 'comes in the name of the Lord'.
- He went to the Temple to drive out those who buy and sell animals. This led to debates with the Jewish authorities and further conflict.
- After His Last Supper with His disciples, Jesus was betrayed by Judas to the authorities. Jesus was tried, found guilty, crucified and resurrected three days later.

Quick Test

1. What happened when John baptised Jesus?
2. What happened at Caesarea Philippi?
3. Who betrayed Jesus?

Key Words

disciple
Transfiguration

Miracles

You must be able to:

- Explore the miracles in Mark's Gospel
- Understand the different types of miracle and their relevance.

> ### Key Scripture and Religious Teaching
>
> Mark 1:32–34, 'That evening after sunset the people brought to Jesus all the sick and demon-possessed. The whole town gathered at the door, and Jesus healed many who had various diseases. He also drove out many demons, but he would not let the demons speak because they knew who he was.'

What are Miracles?

- A **miracle** is a supernatural event outside the usual range of human experience.
- Miracles defy scientific explanation.
- In Mark, miracles are called 'deeds of power' (Greek, 'dynamis').
- They are an expression of Jesus' authority and power.
- Jesus performed miracles in response to faith.
- Some miracles demonstrated Jesus' power over nature; others were an example of His **compassion**.
- They were a tangible sign of the Good News.
- Mark records Jesus performing a variety of miracles: healing miracles and **exorcisms**, nature miracles and resurrections.

Key Point

Jesus healed people, cast out unclean spirits, demonstrated power over nature and raised people from the dead.

Healings and Exorcisms

- Jesus often healed people as a result of their faith or of the faith of others:
  - The woman with internal bleeding (5:25–34);
  - The leper (1:40–45);
  - The deaf and mute man (7:31–37);
  - Simon's mother-in-law (1:30–31);
  - The blind man at Bethsaida (8:22–26);
  - The blind men near Jericho (10:46–52).
- Sometimes, they were a proof of His claim to authority:
  - The paralysed man (2:1–12);
  - The withered hand (3:1–6).
- Mark has several stories where Jesus demonstrates His power over unclean spirits:
  - The man with an unclean spirit (1:23–27);
  - The man with demons (5:1–20).

Key Point

Jesus' miracles were often performed in response to the faith of others.

- And exorcisms as a result of the request of others include:
  - the boy with a demon (9:14–29);
  - the Syrian Phoenician's daughter (7:24–30).

Resurrections

- Although there are several resurrections in the Gospels, there is only one in Mark:
  - The raising of Jairus's daughter (5:21–43) began as a healing in response to faith;
  - By the time Jesus arrived, the girl was dead, but was then raised by Jesus, responding to faith.

Nature Miracles

- There were various occasions where Jesus demonstrated His power over nature.
- Sometimes they were as a result of His compassion for others:
  - Stilling the storm (4:35–41);
  - Feeding the five thousand (6:30–46);
  - Walking on water (6:47–56);
  - Feeding the four thousand (8:1–9);
  - Withering the fig tree (11:20–25).

Quick Test

1. Describe the three main types of miracle in Mark.
2. Why did Jesus perform miracles?
3. What is an exorcism?
4. Define the term 'nature miracle'.
5. Why did Jesus feed the four thousand and the five thousand?

Key Words

miracle
compassion
exorcism
resurrection

The Passion

You must be able to:

- Investigate the opposition of the Jewish authorities in Mark's Gospel
- Explore the events of the last days in Jesus' life.

Key Scripture and Religious Teaching

Mark 16:6, "'Don't be alarmed," he said. "You are looking for Jesus the Nazarene, who was crucified. He has risen! He is not here. See the place where they laid him.'"

Conflict with the Authorities

- The authorities had many conflicts with Jesus throughout His ministry and these are recorded in Mark's Gospel.
- The Pharisees had issues with:
  - His authority (1:22) (11:28);
  - blasphemy (claiming He could forgive sins, as God) (2:1–12);
  - His disciples not fasting (2:18–20);
  - lack of Sabbath observance (2:23–28);
  - healing on the Sabbath (3:1–6);
  - marriage and divorce (10:1–12);
  - cleansing the Temple (11:15–19);
  - paying taxes to the Emperor (12:13–17).
- The Sadducees took issue over His views on resurrection (12:18–27).

> **Key Point**
>
> The Jewish authorities were often in opposition to Jesus.

Arrival in Jerusalem

- On Palm Sunday, Jesus rode on a donkey into Jerusalem, where He was hailed as one who 'comes in the name of the Lord'. People celebrated by scattering palm branches in front of Him.
- He went to the Temple to drive out those who buy and sell animals. This event led to the chief priests and teachers of the law looking for a way to kill Him. Later, they challenged His authority as He walked in the Temple.
- After further arguments with the authorities, Jesus predicted the destruction of the Temple and the end times.

The Last Supper

- After the anointing at Bethany, Jesus celebrated Passover on Thursday evening with His disciples in the Upper Room.
- He warned them of the coming betrayal by one of the 12.

- He shared the bread and wine with them and announced that the bread was His body and the wine was His blood of the covenant.
- Peter promised loyalty when Jesus predicted that he would deny Him three times.

Arrest and Trials

- After supper, they went to the Garden of Gethsemane, on the Mount of Olives, to pray.
- Jesus, deeply distressed, prayed that the cup (of suffering) might be taken away. However, He accepted the coming suffering if it was the will of His Father.
- Despite Jesus' request that they watch and pray, the disciples repeatedly fail to do so.
- Judas betrayed Him to the Jews with a kiss.
- During the trial before the Sanhedrin, Jesus confirmed that He was the Messiah.
- They condemned Him to death because of this blasphemy.
- As they took Jesus to Pilate, Peter denied Jesus three times.
- Pilate condemned Jesus to death as 'King of the Jews', a charge of treason against Rome.

Crucifixion

- After being abused by soldiers, Jesus was taken for crucifixion.
- Simon of Cyrene was forced to carry His cross to Golgotha, the place of execution. Jesus was crucified between two criminals.
- There was darkness between noon and three o'clock.
- Jesus cried out: 'Eloi, Eloi, lama sabachthani?' ('My God, my God, why have you forsaken me?'); and with a loud cry, He died.
- The Temple curtain was torn in two from top to bottom.
- Some of the women watched as His body was placed in a tomb donated by Joseph of Arimathea.

Resurrection

- The women who had seen where Jesus was buried, found the tomb empty when they returned on Sunday morning (after the end of the Sabbath).
- A young man in a white robe said that Jesus had risen and gone before them to Galilee.
- They were instructed to tell the disciples and Peter.
- Further resurrection narratives in Mark 16:9–20 do not appear in the earliest manuscripts and may have been added later.

Quick Test

1. Why were the Jewish authorities opposed to Jesus?
2. What happened when Jesus entered Jerusalem?
3. Describe what happened at the Last Supper.

Key Point

The disciples frequently failed Jesus.

Key Point

The last week of Jesus' life is remembered during Passion Week (Holy Week). It begins on Palm Sunday and includes Maundy Thursday, Good Friday and Holy Saturday.

Key Words

Pharisees
blasphemy
Sanhedrin
crucifixion

How Can the Qur'an Guide Islamic Life?

You must be able to:

- Explore the importance of the Qur'an for believers.
- Investigate what the Qur'an teaches about Allah and His creation.

Key Scripture and Religious Teaching

Qur'an 20:8, 'Allah! There is no god but He! To Him belong the Most Beautiful Names.'

Hadith, Book 35, Number 6475, 'Prophet Muhammad (peace be upon him) said: "To God belongs 99 names (100 minus 1). Anyone who memorizes them will enter Paradise."'

The Nature of Allah

- Surah Al-Fatiha literally means 'The Opening'; this prayer plays a key role in Islam and is a prayer for guidance and mercy.
- Allah is described as being Most Gracious and Most Merciful and is to be worshipped. He cherishes and sustains the worlds and is worthy of all praise.
- Believers seek Allah's help to find the 'straight way', which is for those on whom Allah has bestowed His grace.
- Surah Al-Anaan 13–24 teach about Tawhid and shirk:
  - Tawhid is a fundamental concept in Islam, stating that God is one and single; He is omniscient, omnipotent and transcendent. Tawhid is concerned with the 'oneness of Allah'. There will be no 'Walee' (protector) other than Allah, the Creator of the heavens and the Earth: for Muslims, there must be no other god but Allah.
  - The sin of associating others with Allah is known as shirk, which is the opposite of Tawhid. It is often found in the form of idolatry, believing others to be equal to Allah.
- Muhammad taught that Allah has 99 names, e.g. Ar-Rahman (the Compassionate), Al-Aziz (the Almighty) and Al-Rahim (the Most Merciful). Reciting the names can help Muslims develop their awareness of Allah.

Key Point

Tawhid is Islam's most fundamental concept.

The Nature of Humanity and Believers

- Surah Al-Baqarah is the longest chapter in the Qur'an. It contains 286 verses and covers many topics, describing those who fear Allah, those who reject Islam and hypocrites.
- Mankind is urged to worship Allah and not false gods.

- Disbelievers are warned of the torment of the fires fuelled by mankind. Believers are given the good news of future rewards.
- The Surah frequently reminds people of Allah, the Creator.

Creation

- The Qur'an recounts how, after being joined as 'one unit of creation', the Earth and skies were separated.
- The process of creation took six days.
- Adam sprang to life after he was moulded from clay, earth, sand and water and had life breathed into him.
- Adam and Eve lived in paradise but were expelled as a result of eating forbidden fruit.
- The Qur'an identifies the serpent Shaitan (Satan) as the tempter.

Key Point

The creation stories found throughout the Qur'an are similar to those in Judaism and Christianity.

Justice

- Surah An-Nisa outlines acceptable behaviour for Muslims.
- The Surah examines how to deal fairly with children and orphans. It covers issues about dealing fairly with orphan girls and the practice of marrying orphan girls in order to take their property.
- It discusses inheritance and marriage laws.
- When discussing war, it encourages the Muslim community to fight for the vulnerable.

Lesser Jihad

- The literal meaning of jihad is 'struggle' or 'effort'.
- Muhammad told his followers returning from a battle: 'This day we have returned from the Lesser Jihad to the Greater Jihad,' i.e. returning from armed battle to the peaceful battle for self-control.
- If Lesser Jihad is necessary to protect the faith, anything from legal, diplomatic and political means can be used. However, this is governed by very strict rules, e.g. innocents must never be harmed, and peaceful advances from the enemy must be accepted.
- Lesser Jihad is sometimes referred to as 'holy war'.

Sharia Law

- The whole of a Muslim's life is governed by Sharia. It is the body of Islamic law that governs both public and some private aspects of life.
- The term 'Sharia' literally means 'the path to a watering hole'.
- The purpose of Sharia is to see the will of Allah done on Earth.
- The will of Allah can be known by studying the revealed scriptures.
- Sharia is intended to bring justice rather than tyranny.

Key Point

Sharia law has several sources but is based mainly on the Qur'an and the Hadith.

 Quick Test

1. What does Surah Al-Fatiha teach about Allah?
2. What does Surah Al-Baqarah teach about a Muslim's future?
3. What is meant by 'Greater' and 'Lesser' Jihad?

Key Words

Tawhid
shirk
jihad

What Have the Islamic Prophets Declared About Allah?

You must be able to:

- Explore the lives of the Islamic prophets
- Discover their relevance for Muslims today.

Key Scripture and Religious Teaching

Surah 4 (An-Nisa), 'All who obey Allah and the messenger are in the company of those on whom is the Grace of Allah – of the prophets … Ah! What a beautiful fellowship!'

Nuh

- Nuh (Noah) preached 'submission' (Islam) and warned the people of the impending disaster. He said that the flood could not be delayed and called them to worship the one true God instead of idols.
- Nuh was commanded to build a ship, the Ark, and load it with pairs of every animal available.
- Those who denied his message, including one of his sons, drowned.

Ibrahim

- Ibrahim (Abraham) is mentioned frequently in the Qur'an.
- As a young man, he warned his father and the people to stop worshipping idols and worship only God.
- He is credited with establishing the Ka'ba in Mecca as a place of pilgrimage.

Sulaiman

- According to the Qur'an, Sulaiman was the son of Dawud and a king of Israel.
- Islam views him as a prophet and a divinely appointed king, having received many God-given gifts.

Isa

- Isa (Jesus) is considered to be a messenger of God.
- He was sent to guide the Jews with a new scripture (the gospel).
- He was born by virginal conception, according to the will of Allah.
- He was the only prophet in Islam who could perform miracles.

Key Point

In the Qur'an, Islam is often referred to as 'the religion of Ibrahim' and Ibrahim is known as Khalil-Allah (Friend of God).

Key Point

Sulaiman is one of the most popular holy figures in Islam.

Key Point

Islam considers Isa to be a Muslim who taught his followers to follow the straight path. Islam accepts that Jesus is a prophet but not divine, appearing in 93 ayah (verses).

- He never married nor had children, making him the only such prophet in Islam. Isa did not die (unlike in the Gospels) but ascended bodily into heaven.

Ismail

- Ismail (Ishmael) was Ibrahim's son, born to Hagar.
- Islam holds that Ismail was almost sacrificed by Ibrahim.
- During Eid al-Adha, Muslims slaughter an animal to remember this and remind themselves of the sacrifice in serving Allah.
- In Islam, Ismail is an ancestor to Muhammad and is seen as a prophet. He was associated with Mecca and was involved with the construction of the Ka'ba (right).

Yusuf

- Islam holds that Yusuf was given the gift of prophecy.
- The story is contained in only one surah, making it unique.
- Yusuf's story is very similar to the biblical account.
- He is described as having three key characteristics: pastoral ability, household management and self-control.

Musa

- Musa's and Muhammad's lives are often considered to be parallel.
- He is venerated as 'Kalim Allah': the one who talked with God.
- He received the Tawrat (Torah), described in the Qur'an as 'guidance and a light', with teachings about the oneness of God.

> **Key Point**
>
> The stories of Yusuf and Musa in the Qur'an are very similar to the biblical accounts.

Dawud

- Dawud (David) is famous in Islam for defeating Goliath.
- He is recognised as a messenger, prophet and law-giver.
- The story of Dawud in the Qur'an is similar to the biblical account, although Muslims do not accept the sins of adultery and murder attributed to him.
- Dawud is important because he was given the Zabur (Psalms).
- He is one of the few Islamic prophets to also be king.

Maryam

- Maryam (Mary) is given more attention in the Qur'an than any other woman. Surah 19 of the Qur'an is named after her.
- There are stories about her birth, early life, as well as the biblical stories of the birth of Isa (Jesus).
- She is specifically mentioned as a role model for believers.

> **Key Point**
>
> Maryam is mentioned more times in the Qur'an than in the New Testament. She is seen as the most righteous woman in Islam and is said to have been a virgin.

 **Quick Test**

1. Why is Ibrahim important to Muslims?
2. What does the Qur'an omit about the life of Dawud?

 Key Words

prophet
prophecy

Does God Exist?

1 Define the term 'monotheistic'. [1]

....

2 What name is given to someone who is unsure of, or yet to decide on, their religious beliefs? [1]

....

3 Define 'eternal' as a characteristic of God. [1]

....

4 Explain the importance of the book of Revelation when studying the nature of God. [4]

....

....

....

....

5 'The existence of God will never be proven.'

Explain three reasons why some may agree with this statement and three reasons why others may disagree with this statement. [6]

....

....

....

....

....

....

....

Total Marks .... / 13

What Do They Believe?

1 Who is the messenger of Allah? [1]

2 Throughout Jewish scripture, what were removed from the name Yahweh? [1]

3 What is the name given to food prepared for Jewish consumption? [1]

4 Explain Muslim beliefs about Allah. [4]

5 'Basing your life upon ancient beliefs is outdated and irrelevant in today's society.'

Explain three reasons why some may agree with this statement and three reasons why others may disagree with this statement. [6]

Total Marks _____ / 13

Review Questions

How Do They Worship?

1. On what day do Muslims attend a mosque to pray? [1]

2. What is the name given to the Jewish holy day? [1]

3. What is the sacred food shared between Sikhs? [1]

4. Describe what acts may be described as worship. [4]

5. 'Worship is important, but the time could be better spent helping others rather than being inside a holy building.'

   Explain three reasons why some may agree with this statement and three reasons why others may disagree with this statement. [6]

Total Marks _____ / 13

What Makes Christian Worship Different?

1 On which day do Christians often worship at church? [1]

....

2 Which festival celebrates the Holy Spirit coming to Earth? [1]

....

3 What piece of furniture is used when the sermon is preached? [1]

....

4 Describe the origins of worship in Christianity. [4]

....

....

....

....

5 'Prayer is the most important part of worship.'

Explain three reasons why some may agree with this statement and three reasons why others may disagree with this statement. [6]

....

....

....

....

....

....

Total Marks .... / 13

Review Questions

How Does Scripture Guide Christian Life?

1 How do many Christians describe the Bible? [1]

2 What is detailed throughout the book of the Acts of the Apostles? [1]

3 Explain how the Bible can guide a Christian's moral decision-making. [4]

4 'The differences between the four Gospels show that they are not accurate and brings into question the existence of Jesus.'

Explain three reasons why some may agree with this statement and three reasons why others may disagree with this statement. [6]

Total Marks _____ / 12

Other Scriptures

1 How did Muhammad receive the Qur'an? [1]

_____

2 What are the first five books of the Tenakh known as? [1]

_____

3 Who was the last author of the Guru Granth Sahib? [1]

_____

4 Describe the nature of how the Tenakh is written and used. [4]

_____

_____

_____

_____

5 Describe how the Guru Granth Sahib is treated and why it is treated this way. [6]

_____

_____

_____

_____

_____

_____

Total Marks _____ / 13

Review Questions

How Do They Live Their Lives?

1 What laws govern the eating of meat in Judaism? [1]

....

2 What ceremony does a Jewish boy pass through as he grows up? [1]

....

3 What is the Muslim profession of faith? [1]

....

4 What term governs the treatment of meat for Muslims? What does it mean in terms
of preparing the meat? [2]

....

....

5 Explain how and why Zakah is important to Muslims. [4]

....

....

....

....

6   How can the life of a Christian be shaped by their faith?   [6]

....

....

....

....

....

....

Total Marks .... / 15

Practice Questions

Jesus' Teaching

1 Define the term 'Messiah'. [2]

....

....

2 What technique did Jesus often use when teaching? [2]

....

....

3 What does the title 'Son of Man' suggest about Jesus? [2]

....

....

4 What are the four main themes of Jesus' teaching in Mark's Gospel? [4]

....

....

....

....

5 Suggest reasons why Jesus refused to call Himself the 'Son of God' until His trial. [5]

....

....

....

....

....

....

Total Marks .... / 15

Ministry of Jesus

1 What does it mean to be a 'disciple'? [2]

2 Give two characteristics of Mark's Gospel. [2]

3 How does Mark describe Jesus in chapter 1? [2]

4 Why did Jesus call the disciples that He did? [4]

5 Describe the events of the Transfiguration. [5]

Total Marks .... / 15

Miracles

1 Define the word 'miracle'. [2]

_____

_____

2 Name two types of miracle. [2]

_____

_____

3 What are resurrections? [2]

_____

_____

4 Name four nature miracles from Mark's Gospel. [4]

_____

_____

_____

_____

5 Why are the miracles found in Mark important to Christians? [5]

_____

_____

_____

_____

_____

Total Marks _____ / 15

The Passion

1 Define the term 'blasphemy'. [2]

....

....

2 In which passages does Jesus challenge the Pharisees about authority? [2]

....

....

3 Give two key details of Palm Sunday. [2]

....

....

4 How are the events of the Last Supper remembered today? [4]

....

....

....

....

5 What are some of the key events of Jesus' crucifixion? [5]

....

....

....

....

....

Total Marks .... / 15

How Can the Qur'an Guide Islamic Life?

1. What is proclaimed in 20:8 of the Qur'an? [2]

2. What are the two jihads in Islam and what do they mean? [2]

3. What is Sharia law? [2]

4. What does the Qur'an teach about creation? [4]

5. How does the Qur'an describe Allah? [5]

Total Marks _____ / 15

What Have the Islamic Prophets Declared About Allah?

1 Who was Nuh (Noah)? [2]

_____

_____

2 What is Ibrahim recorded as being responsible for? [2]

_____

_____

3 Who was Sulaiman and what is his connection to Judaism? [2]

_____

_____

4 Who is the most important woman in the Qur'an and what defines her importance? [4]

_____

_____

_____

_____

5 How does the Qur'an portray Isa (Jesus)? [5]

_____

_____

_____

_____

_____

Total Marks _____ / 15

How Can Christians Experience God?

You must be able to:

- Explore the nature and importance of visions and miracles from the Bible
- Understand the variety of miracles found in the New Testament
- Describe the nature of near-death experiences.

Key Scripture and Religious Teaching

John 2:7–8, 'Jesus said to the servants, "Fill the jars with water"; so they filled them to the brim. Then he told them, "Now draw some out and take it to the master of the banquet."'

Revelation 1:1–2, 'The revelation of Jesus Christ, which God gave him to show his servants what must soon take place. He made it known by sending his angel to his servant John, who testifies to everything he saw – that is, the word of God and the testimony of Jesus Christ.'

Nature Miracles

- Throughout the New Testament, Jesus showed His power over creation by controlling the laws of physics in numerous ways.
- Jesus showed this power over the elements of weather and also through the use of food and drink.
- Jesus' first **nature miracle** appears in John 2:1–11, as He turns jugs full of water into wine.
- In Matthew 8:23–27, Jesus and the disciples are caught in a storm on Lake Galilee.
- Jesus is woken by the disciples and commands the waves and weather to be calmed.
- When preaching to one of his largest crowds in Matthew 14:13–21, Jesus is informed by the disciples that the crowd are hungry.
- A young boy offers five loaves of bread and two fish to Jesus, who then blesses the food to feed the 5000 men, with 12 baskets of food left over.

Healing Miracles

- The New Testament also features accounts of Jesus overcoming human illness and disability.
- Jesus' first **healing miracle** appears in John 4:46–54, when He healed a royal official's son.
- In Matthew 9:1–8, a paralysed man is lowered through a roof into a room where Jesus is sitting.
- Jesus forgives the man his sins and commands him to 'get up and walk', healing him in the process.

Key Point

The Bible contains accounts of many experiences of God and revelations of His power through visions and miracles.

- One of Jesus' most remarkable miracles is the moment when He raised Lazarus from the dead.
- John 11:1–44 sees Jesus visiting Lazarus' tomb four days after his death.
- Jesus commands Lazarus to leave the tomb, whereupon he appears in front of the crowd wearing his linen burial cloths.

Visions in the Bible

- Visions of God and from God appear throughout the Bible from Genesis to Revelation.
- God appears to Abraham on numerous occasions, and in Genesis 15:1–5 God says He will protect him and promises him that he will have many descendants, despite his age.
- Later, God speaks to His prophets, notably revealing His desire for Jonah to speak to the people of Nineveh.
- Early in the New Testament, some Christians believe God reveals Himself to Joseph in Matthew 1:20 to tell him of the coming birth of Jesus.

The Book of Revelation

- The book of Revelation is the last book of the Bible and different from all other books, as it is an account of John's visions from God.
- John sees the events at the end of the world and the second coming of Christ.
- The book reveals how the world will come to an end and how a new world will be created.

Near-Death Experiences

- There have been many accounts of people being close to death and experiencing something of the afterlife.
- These near-death experiences are visions that often share commonalities, such as seeing memories of the past and a tunnel with a bright light at the end.
- Near-death experiences are often used as evidence for the existence of God and the afterlife.
- Ian McCormack was an atheist who was stung by box jellyfish. While on his hospital bed, he had an out-of-body experience and believed that he saw his mother, hell and heaven while unconscious.
- Ian made a miraculous and full recovery, became a committed Christian and now travels the world sharing his story.

> **Key Point**
>
> Christians believe that visions and miracles still happen today.

> **Key Words**
>
> nature miracles
> healing miracles
> vision
> near-death experience

> **Quick Test**
>
> 1. What are the differences between healing and nature miracles?
> 2. How is the book of Revelation different to the others in the Bible?
> 3. What is common in a near-death experience?

How Can Life Be Sacred?

You must be able to:

- Describe the nature of the sanctity of life
- Understand why human life is holy and how this is shown in the Bible
- Consider the implications of the sanctity of life when looking at ethical issues.

> ### Key Scripture and Religious Teaching
>
> Genesis 1:31, 'God saw all that he had made, and it was very good.'
>
> John 3:16, 'For God so loved the world that he gave his one and only Son, that whoever believes in him shall not perish but have eternal life.'

What Does the 'Sanctity of Life' Mean?

- The principle of sanctity of life is the concept that life is precious, created and given by God.
- As life is created by God, it has an intrinsic value and is sacred.
- As God creates life, only God should take life away, and humans should aim to protect each other's lives and wellbeing.

> ### Key Point
>
> If life is created by God, then only God or nature should cause a life to end.

Humans and the Creation

- On the sixth day of the creation, God had completed the universe except for the creatures to dwell on the land.
- Once God had created animals, He announced that humans were to be created in His own image.
- Humanity was separated from the rest of creation and placed in a position of authority over it (stewardship).
- Many Christians believe that a key aspect of this separation is the intrinsic value that is given to humans through the soul.

Sanctity of Life in the Bible

- There are numerous references to life in the Bible, with many pointing to the value of life.
- Jeremiah 1:5: 'Before I formed you in the womb I knew you, before you were born I set you apart; I appointed you as a prophet to the nations.'
- The verse emphasises the importance of human life by revealing that God knows each human before they have even been born.
- God's control over the creation of human life is further revealed in Job 12:10, 'In his hand is the life of every living thing and the breath of all mankind'. This verse highlights the belief that all life is created by God, having intrinsic value, and that God sustains all life.

- Arguably the most well-known verse in the Bible is John 3:16, 'For God so loved the world, that He gave his only Son, that whoever believes in Him should not perish but have eternal life'.
- The death and resurrection of Jesus underpins much of the Christian faith.
- If God was willing to sacrifice the life of His own son to save mankind, it is easy to argue that the sanctity of life is revealed.

What is the Role of the Soul?

- The soul is the eternal aspect of our lives that contains the essence of who we are.
- Some Christians believe that, when we die, our human existence ends but the soul lives on into the afterlife. Others believe we are physically resurrected after we die.
- Some Christians believe we are judged on the way we live our lives.
- For Christians, they could either live on in heaven, purgatory or hell.

Sanctity of Life and War

- In times of war, civilians and service personnel lose their lives.
- Joining an armed force comes with the knowledge that your life will be at risk and you may have to take the life of others.
- The decision to join the armed forces can raise questions over the value of life and can lead many Christians to either be a pacifist or to become a conscientious objector.

Abortion and Ending a Life

- Abortion is the premature termination of a pregnancy and in the UK is allowed, with certain stipulations, no later than 24 weeks, barring two exceptions.
- Clarifying when a human life begins can play a big part in decisions about whether abortions should happen or not.
- Muslim views depend upon at what stage of the pregnancy the abortion is planned for, but the decision is still not taken lightly. It is further complicated if the pregnancy has passed 120 days.
- Historically, suicide was illegal in the UK. The law recognised that the ending of life was immoral, even if it was your own.
- It is now recognised that an individual should be supported and helped, rather than punished, if they want to end their life.
- With advances in medicine, we have the ability to humanely end life through euthanasia (see pages 108–109), but the ethical issues behind the ending of a human life remain.

 Key Point

Belief in the sanctity of life is at the heart of many of today's key ethical issues.

Quick Test
1. On what day were humans created?
2. In whose image were humans created?
3. Describe the soul.

 Key Words

sanctity of life
intrinsic
sacred
abortion

Sanctity of Life

You must be able to:

- Explore religious views of the origins of life.

Key Scripture and Religious Teaching

Genesis 1:27, 'So God created man in His own image, in the image of God He created Him; male and female He created them.'

1 Corinthians 3:16, 'Don't you know that your body is the temple of the Holy Spirit and that God lives in you?'

Psalm 139:13, 'For you created my inmost being; you knit me together in my mother's womb.'

Christian View of the Sanctity of Life

- UK law recognises that life begins at birth and does not grant human rights status until birth.
- Most Christians believe that life begins at the moment the sperm fertilises the egg (conception) and the soul has been given to the embryo.
- Christians believe that God created all things and He has therefore created each life.
- As He is the Creator, only He has the right to end life, making it sacred.
- It is also the responsibility of humanity to try to protect the life of each human.
- Both Jews and Christians believe that humans were created separately from the rest of creation (on the sixth day) and have been made in God's image.
- The passage in Genesis 1 also states that males and females are equal as they were both created in His image.
- Genesis 2:7 reads, '(God) breathed into his nostrils the breath of life'.
- Christians believe that if God was willing to sacrifice the life of His own son to save mankind, human life must be precious to Him.

Key Point

All religions believe that God has created life.

Key Point

Only God has the right to take life away.

Muslim View of the Sanctity of Life

- Muslims believe that the sanctity of life is a key part of their faith.
- Life begins when the ruh (soul) is given to the foetus.
- Some Muslims believe that this occurs at 40 days, some at 120 days and others when there is voluntary movement of the foetus.
- Once this has occurred, the foetus is a real human and is protected by Islam.
- Qur'an 5:32 reads, 'Whosoever has spared the life of a soul, it is as though he has spared the life of all people. Whosoever has killed a soul, it is as though he has murdered all of mankind.'
- Muslims believe that life is given by Allah and should be both respected and protected because of this.

Jewish View of the Sanctity of Life

- Judaism has a supreme concern for the sanctity of human life.
- For Jews, a foetus in the womb is considered a human life 'under construction'.
- However, some Jews argue that life is fully granted after 40 days of the pregnancy.
- Traditionally, they believe that the soul arrives 'when the first breath of life is taken' at birth.
- There are numerous references to life in Jewish scriptures with many pointing to the sanctity of life.
- Mishnah, Sanhedrin 4:5, 'Whoever destroys one life is as if he destroyed a whole world, and whoever preserves a life is as if he preserved the whole world.'
- In Jeremiah 1:5 it states, 'Before I formed you in the womb I knew you, and before you were born I consecrated you; I appointed you a prophet to the nations.'
- God knows each human before they have even been born, so every life is important.

Sikh View of the Sanctity of Life

- Sikhs have great respect for life, which is regarded as a gift from Waheguru.
- They too believe that life should be protected wherever possible and that it is the greatest gift given to them.

Quick Test

1. What scriptures may Christians use to support their views about God creating life?
2. When do Jews believe that life begins?
3. When do Muslims believe that life begins?

Key Words

ruh

Birth Matters

You must be able to:

- Investigate religious views on abortion
- Explore the issues involved with embryology and in vitro fertilisation (IVF).

Key Scripture and Religious Teaching

Jeremiah 1:5, 'Before I formed you in the womb I knew you, before you were born I set you apart.'

Psalm 139:13, 'For you created my inmost being; you knit me together in my mother's womb.'

When Does Life Begin?

- Most Christians, Muslims and Jews believe that God is present and involved in the creation of life.
- However, there are different views as to when life actually begins (see pages 98–99).
- UK law recognises that life starts at birth.
- The question of when life begins has many ethical implications.

In Vitro Fertilisation

- During **in vitro** fertilisation (IVF), the egg is fertilised with either the partner's sperm or that of a donor in a laboratory.
- In artificial insemination by husband (AIH) the man may have a low sperm count or other complications exist but his sperm are still healthy.
- In artificial insemination by donor (AID) the male partner is unable to provide suitable sperm for a pregnancy to take place, so a third party donates the sperm.
- In the UK, most couples are able to have their first treatment at the expense of the NHS but then have to pay for further treatments if this is unsuccessful.
- The Christian Church has responded clearly to the ethical discussion on IVF, although different branches give different guidance. However, all have explained that IVF is suitable in some circumstances but not in all.
- Muslims only support AIH, as they feel that the involvement of a third party undermines the marriage.
- Some Jews believe that IVF offers couples a chance to be blessed by God and therefore is absolutely necessary for a couple if it is available and should not be turned down.

Key Point

When life starts has a big influence on religious views concerning matters such as abortion.

Key Point

Western religions believe that all life comes from God.

Embryology

- **Embryology** is the use of embryos in scientific research to try to find cures for diseases and illnesses. It is governed by strict laws.
- The Embryology Act (1990) allowed scientists to create embryos outside of the womb and store them legally for the first time.
- In 2008, women were given the right to donate their eggs to scientific research, raising questions about the 'potential' of life.
- Many religious believers would argue that life is not being protected or valued in the way that a gift from God should be.
- In the UK, embryos are only allowed to be tested on up to the 14th day.

Abortion

- UK laws on abortion have remained relatively unchanged since the Abortion Act of 1967 was passed (although the time limit has now been reduced from 28 weeks to 24 weeks).
- The bill set out guidelines as to when an abortion can be allowed and on what grounds. These rules apply up to the first 24 weeks of a pregnancy. From this point on, abortions are usually only allowed in extreme cases.
- One such case is that of a 'strong likelihood of a severe disability'. Some, including believers, would support this with the 'Quality of Life' argument, believing it better not to allow a baby to be born whose standard of living would be poor.
- Some Christians believe this to be the most compassionate decision, whilst others believe that God can use life as a blessing, whatever the circumstances.
- Whether an individual believes life begins at conception, 40 days or at 120 days, the question about whether that life should be terminated raises the issue of the sanctity of life.
- As many Christians and Jews believe that life begins at conception, abortion at any stage should be avoided, perhaps with the exception of protecting the life of the mother (this is one circumstance where abortion is allowed after 24 weeks).
- Muslim views depend upon at what stage of the pregnancy the abortion is planned for, but the decision is still not taken lightly. It is further complicated if the pregnancy has passed 120 days.
- 'Pro Life' campaigners argue against abortion, saying that an unwanted pregnancy should not be terminated but, when born, the baby should be given up for adoption.
- 'Pro Choice' supporters focus their beliefs and arguments on the rights of the mother and not those of the foetus.

> ### Key Point
>
> In the UK, two doctors must agree for an abortion to be legal, unless it is a medical emergency. A woman can make a request for an abortion without discussing it with her partner or family.

> ### Key Words
>
> **in vitro**
> **embryology**
> **conception**

Quick Test

1. Why might embryology cause concern for believers?
2. Describe the different types of IVF.
3. Why do believers often have problems concerning abortion?

Marriage and Divorce

You must be able to:

- Explore the different types of marriage ceremony
- Investigate the different approaches to divorce.

> ### Key Scripture and Religious Teaching
>
> Mark 10:6–8, 'In the beginning God created them male and female. For this reason a man shall leave his father and mother and be joined to his wife, and the two shall become one flesh.'

Getting Married

- Marriage is a contract that binds a couple together in the eyes of the law.
- Religious marriage gives the couple the opportunity to make their promises before God.
- Although different faiths have different ceremonies, they all emphasise the centrality of these promises.
- Many believe that God intended children to be born within the secure environment of a committed marriage, thus resulting in many faiths teaching that sex before marriage should not occur.

> ### Key Point
>
> All faiths emphasise the centrality of the promises made in marriage.

Christian Marriage

- Christians believe that marriage was God's plan from creation, visible in the relationship of Adam and Eve.
- Traditionally, a Christian bride wears white to symbolise purity.
- The ceremony includes hymns, prayers and scriptures.
- Promises are made and vows are said in front of family and friends. Rings are exchanged that symbolise the eternal nature of marriage.
- After a sermon and blessing, a legally-binding marriage certificate is signed.
- A reception and honeymoon usually follow the ceremony.

Muslim Marriage

- Traditionally, Muslim marriages are arranged marriages.
- The interests of the woman are safeguarded by a legal contract, which provides a financial settlement (mahr) from the husband.
- There is a simple ceremony (called a nikah) with the Qur'an being read and a sermon being preached by the imam.
- Vows are exchanged before witnesses and a ring may be given.

- A white wedding dress is common, but Asian brides often favour the shalwar-kameez.
- A celebration usually follows the ceremony.

Jewish Marriage

- With the exception of the Sabbath or a major festival, Jewish weddings can take place on any day, often in a synagogue.
- The marriage takes place under the chuppah (right).
- The service is conducted by a rabbi and begins with the signing of the ketubah by the couple and two witnesses.
- Prayers will be said and glasses of wine drunk. Scriptures are read, rings exchanged, blessings given and a glass broken under foot.
- The groom wears black and the bride white.
- There is a reception after the ceremony.

Sikh Marriage

- Sikh marriage ceremonies can take place on any suitable day and are usually held in the morning in a Gurdwara.
- Traditionally, the man wears white and the woman wears red.
- The couple sit in the presence of the Guru Granth Sahib, and hymns are sung.
- A baptised Sikh performs the marriage and begins by explaining the duties of married life. The couple bow before the book to show their acceptance of this.
- The bridegroom wears a sash over his shoulder which is placed in the bride's hands.
- Verses are read from the Granth and the couple walk around the book – the groom leading the bride – to the singing of hymns. This is repeated four times.
- After further readings from the Granth, Kara Parshad is eaten by all present. Following the ceremony, a wedding banquet takes place.

Divorce

- The Protestant denomination accepts divorce and remarriage.
- The Catholic Church does not allow divorce or remarriage. However, an annulment is sometimes granted.
- Divorce is possible for Muslims, but the couple must have tried to reconcile for three months first. Muslims can re-marry.
- Jews accept that divorce and remarriage may occur.
- Divorce is a taboo in Sikhism, with many arguing that it should not be allowed.

Key Point

Christian denominations have different views about divorce and remarriage.

Quick Test

1. What do Christian, Muslim and Jewish marriages have in common?
2. What is the Catholic Church's view of divorce and remarriage?

Key Words

shalwar-kameez
chuppah
ketubah
annulment

Is Family More Important Than Friends?

You must be able to:

- Understand the nature of families in society
- Describe and explain the structure of different family groups including nuclear, single parent, same-sex parents, extended and blended families
- Explain the benefits and challenges of each family group.

Key Scripture and Religious Teaching

Exodus 20:12, 'Honour your father and your mother, so that you may live long in the land the LORD your God is giving you.'

Ephesians 6:4, 'Fathers, do not exasperate your children; instead, bring them up in the training and instruction of the LORD.'

Proverbs 6:20, 'My son, keep your father's commands and do not forsake your mother's teaching.'

The Role of Family in Society

- Despite 'family' now meaning many things around the world, it is still central to society. It does not just refer to people living under the same roof.
- Families should provide an education for the next generation that cannot be delivered in the classroom. They are responsible for creating the first experiences that any child has.
- Older members of a family group can lead a child into a religion and broaden their knowledge of religious beliefs.
- In the community, families can work together with other families to create a sense of unity, whether they are religious or not.
- If a society is made up of stable family groups, then a society is much more likely to be at peace with itself, e.g. Sodom and Gomorrah are classic biblical examples of what happens when this is not the case.

The Role of Family in Christianity

- Husbands and wives have distinct responsibilities within the family unit both for themselves and towards each other.
- Traditionally the husband would be the 'breadwinner' for the family, while the wife would stay at home to bring up the children and look after the home; but now both often work.
- Although seen much less in modern society, the husband was considered to be the head of the family and largely responsible for decisions made in the house.

Key Point

Family can take many different shapes and forms, but all are of equal value.

- Ephesians 5:22–25 recounts examples of how husbands should love and care for their wives and how wives should submit to their husbands.
- The concept of submission is less common in today's society, arguably due to its abuse throughout history.
- However, in Galatians 3:28, Paul explains how men and women are equal, suggesting a greater sense of shared responsibility in the family.
- Having and raising children is often seen as a central purpose to a Christian marriage, illustrated by the instruction in Genesis 1:28 to the first couple to 'be fruitful and multiply'.

How are Family Groups Different?

- Family can take on many different shapes and sizes.
- The nuclear family focuses on the immediate relationship of the father, mother and children.
- However, this group may be based around a heterosexual couple, a homosexual couple or a single parent of either gender.
- In religion, an extended family can include grandparents and aunts and uncles, sometimes living under the same roof.
- With divorce common in society, some family units are blended, with children from different parents living together with one parent, their step-parent and step-siblings.

How is a Religious Family Different to a Secular One?

- In many respects, the religious family is very similar to a secular one.
- With many marriages failing and ending in divorce in secular society, it is more likely to find a married couple at the centre of a Christian family.
- This may not be the case in a secular family, with the couple either cohabiting or joined by a civil partnership.
- Single parent families are also not uncommon in Christianity and should not be seen as having a lower status than a two-parent family.
- A religious family may also spend more time together, as they are likely to worship and read scriptures together, e.g. Jews celebrate Shabbat together (right), with each member of the family having roles to play in the ceremony.
- Christian parents are also likely to take their children to church with them and bring them up following the rules of the Bible.

> **Key Point**
>
> Religious families are similar to secular ones in many ways but are responsible for raising their children in the faith.

> **Key Words**
>
> submission
> nuclear family
> blended family

> **Quick Test**
>
> 1. Why are families important?
> 2. How has family changed in recent years?
> 3. In what ways is a religious family different to a secular one?

Are Children the Centre of the Family?

You must be able to:

- Understand the purpose of the family in Christianity
- To explain Church teachings about the nature and purpose of family
- To explain how Christians respond to the changing nature of family life in the 21st century in the UK.

Key Scripture and Religious Teaching

Matthew 19:14, 'Jesus said, "Let the little children come to me, and do not hinder them, for the kingdom of heaven belongs to such as these."'

Psalm 127:3, 'Children are a heritage from the LORD, offspring a reward from him.'

How Can a Christian Be a Good Parent?

- The Bible teaches how Christian parenting follows key responsibilities.
- The majority of Christians believe that children are a gift from God and should be treated with care (Psalm 127:3).
- In addition, some would argue that parents have a role to protect their children and guide their life in Christianity before they can make their own decisions.
- A parent should follow the caring example set by Jesus and the attitude that He had towards children during His life.
- In Matthew 19:14, Jesus looks beyond the crowd in front of Him and encourages the children to come to Him.
- Jesus states that 'the Kingdom of God belongs to the children' and that adults should encourage closeness to God and not limit it – this obviously starts with the parents.

Key Point

Being a good parent as a Christian is the same as being a good parent as a non-Christian – with the addition of bringing the children up in the Christian faith.

Dedication, Infant Baptism and Confirmation

- As part of being a parent, a Christian will often want to thank God for their child in a ceremony called infant baptism.
- In the Protestant and Catholic traditions, children are often baptised, with parents and godparents bringing the child to the priest who conducts the ceremony at the font.
- The priest asks them questions and they make promises about supporting the child in its Christian life.
- Water from the font is sprinkled on the baby's head and the sign of the cross is made. In the Orthodox tradition, the baby is submersed fully under water.

- The priest gives the baby its name and says 'I baptise you in the name of the Father, and of the Son, and of the Holy Spirit'.
- In contrast, some churches practise the rite of dedication.
- Promises are again made by the parents and godparents but no promises are made on behalf of the child.
- Water is also absent from the ceremony and, therefore, so is the font.
- Both ceremonies introduce the child into Christianity while also thanking God for the child.
- When a child is older, parents may guide them towards the confirmation ceremony and the lessons prior to the ceremony.
- During the service, the child will be asked to renew the promises made for them at baptism.
- They then make further promises and the bishop lays hands on them, saying 'receive the Holy Spirit'.
- Prayers are said for them and then they will join the bishop in saying the Apostles' Creed.
- Once they have been confirmed, Holy Communion can be taken. In the Catholic Church, a child may take their first Holy Communion around the age of 7, before they are confirmed at 12–14.

Christian Family Life

- To aid the development of their children, parents will often pray and study the Bible with them.
- This adds to what the children receive during their time at church on a Sunday and can help to guide them in their everyday lives.
- Festivals such as Easter and Pentecost can be celebrated in the home to help children remember the history of their religion.
- Also, at Christmas, services like midnight mass can re-focus attention on the birth of Jesus and away from the commercial aspects of Christmas, including presents.

Key Point

Key ceremonies can mark stages of a child's life that can build their faith.

Points to Consider

- Consider:
  - the statement, 'Parents should not indoctrinate their children with their beliefs but should allow them to make their own decisions';
  - the difference between 'baptism' and 'dedication' and whether either activity is relevant for babies today;
  - at what age it is appropriate for young people to 'confirm' the promises made for them when they were babies.

Quick Test

1. How are infant baptism and dedication different?
2. Think of three ways in which a Christian can be a good parent.
3. In some Church traditions, why do you think a child does not take Holy Communion until after they have been confirmed?

Key Words

parenting
responsibilities
infant baptism
dedication
confirmation

Death and Who Can End Life

You must be able to:

- Explore religious views about death
- Investigate ethical questions about the end of life.

> ### Key Scripture and Religious Teaching
>
> 1 Corinthians 3:16, 'Don't you know that your body is the temple of the Holy Spirit and that God lives in you?'
>
> Job 1:21, 'The LORD gave and the LORD has taken away.'

About Death

- When a Jew dies, the body is dressed in a simple linen shroud and placed in a wooden coffin. From death to burial, the body is never left alone.
- Cremation is generally forbidden.
- The ceremony usually takes place in the synagogue as soon as practically possible, following which the family will 'sit shiva', a mourning period of seven days.
- Christian funerals usually occur about a week after the death.
- The funeral service often takes place in a church, where hymns are sung, passages from the Bible are read and prayers are said.
- After the service, there will be a burial or cremation.
- If the death of a Muslim is expected, the call to prayer is repeated.
- Soon after death, the body is washed and wrapped in a linen shroud.
- Prayers of forgiveness are said for the dead and the body is buried in a grave, parallel with Mecca, with the head facing Mecca.
- Cremation of Muslims is forbidden.
- Sikhs generally cremate people when they die.
- The coffin is placed on a funeral pyre, which is lit by a close relative.

Euthanasia

- Euthanasia is sometimes known as 'mercy killing'.
- UK law is very clear: the removal of treatment that is prolonging life (passive euthanasia) is legal.
- However, any form of active euthanasia is illegal.
- It is also illegal for any UK citizen to help someone else leave the country to go to end their life early in a country where it is legal, such as Switzerland.

> ### Key Point
>
> The major world faiths do not allow active euthanasia.

- Active euthanasia can be both voluntary, where the individual gives their consent, or involuntary, where they do not or cannot.
- The major world religions object to active euthanasia.
- Passive euthanasia can only occur with either the patient's consent, or the consent of the family and the agreement of a doctor.
- Euthanasia should not be confused with 'assisted suicide'.
- Assisted suicide takes place without the guidance of a medical professional and often involves a family member or close friend helping someone to die, though ultimately they have ended their life themselves.
- The hospice movement provides those nearing the end of their lives with the opportunity to make the most of their final days through palliative care.
- Palliative care is medical treatment which seeks to relieve the symptoms and suffering of someone with a terminal illness. It does not seek to cure them.
- Hospices care for people of any age, not just the elderly.

The Death Penalty

- The death penalty is another term for state-sanctioned execution.
- Discussions about the morality of capital punishment revolve around the question of who has the right to take another's life.
- Throughout history, many horrific forms of death penalty have been used.
- These are obviously barbaric in their nature but the development of humane death penalties, such as lethal injection, can raise further moral questions.
- Some have argued that ending the life of a serial murderer is better than the cost of life imprisonment.
- In the UK, the last executions were Peter Anthony Allen at Liverpool's Walton Prison and Gwynne Owen Evans at Manchester's Strangeways Prison. Both were hanged on 13 August, 1964.
- However, some UK citizens have been executed in other countries.
- China executes more people every year than the rest of the world combined. The number of executions in China is estimated at 2000–4000 annually.

> **Key Point**
>
> The death penalty is no longer used in the UK, but it is still used in other countries around the world.

> **Key Words**
>
> passive euthanasia
> active euthanasia
> hospice
> capital punishment

> **Quick Test**
>
> 1. Which religions allow cremation?
> 2. What is euthanasia?
> 3. What is meant by the death penalty?

Review Questions

Jesus' Teaching

1 What is the 'Messianic Secret'? [1]

....

2 What is the key event in Mark 1:16–20? [1]

....

3 What key quality of discipleship is described in Mark 9:35? [1]

....

4 Describe the Parable of the Lamp from Mark 4:21–25. [4]

....

....

....

....

5 'Jesus' teachings were helpful but not a definitive guide for living.'

Explain three reasons why some may agree with this statement and three reasons why others may disagree with this statement. [6]

....

....

....

....

....

....

Total Marks .... / 13

Ministry of Jesus

1. Which disciple doubted Jesus' resurrection? [1]

2. What do you think is meant by the Good News? [1]

3. What was Simon Peter's job before Jesus called him? [1]

4. What suggestions could be given as to why Jesus called 12 disciples? [4]

5. 'As Jesus only called men to be His disciples, He showed that men are superior to women.'

   Explain three reasons why some may agree with this statement and three reasons why others may disagree with this statement. [6]

Total Marks _____ / 13

Review Questions

Miracles

1 What miracle is found in Mark 1:30–31? [1]

2 Why did Jesus' miracles concern the Pharisees? [1]

3 Describe the healing of the deaf and mute man in Mark 7:31–37. [4]

4 'Jesus shouldn't have performed miracles on the Sabbath as He knew that it would anger the Pharisees.'

Explain three reasons why some may agree with this statement and three reasons why others may disagree with this statement. [6]

Total Marks _____ / 12

The Passion

1 What is crucifixion? [1]

....

2 Who betrayed Jesus? [1]

....

3 Which religious court tried Jesus? [1]

....

4 What are the four most significant days during Passion Week? [4]

....

....

....

....

5 'The Passion story is a message of hope rather than a factual account.'

Explain three reasons why some may agree with this statement and three reasons why others may disagree with this statement. [6]

....

....

....

....

....

....

Total Marks .... / 13

How Can the Qur'an Guide Islamic Life?

1 How many names did Muhammad proclaim that Allah had? [1]

2 What Islamic teaching describes the 'oneness' of Allah? [1]

3 What concept dictates that no one should be made equal with Allah? [1]

4 What role does jihad play in the life of a Muslim? [4]

5 'As the Islamic story of creation is so similar to that of Christianity and Judaism, it suggests that the account in the Qur'an may not be accurate.'

Explain three reasons why some may agree with this statement and three reasons why others may disagree with this statement. [6]

Total Marks _____ / 13

What Have the Islamic Prophets Declared About Allah?

1 What task was Nuh given by Allah? [1]

2 What was the fate of those who refused to enter the Ark? [1]

3 What was the name of Ismail's mother? [1]

4 Why do you think Allah sent prophets in addition to the teachings of the Qur'an? [4]

5 'The absence of modern day prophets suggests that Allah has no new teachings for Muslims to follow.'

Explain three reasons why some may agree with this statement and three reasons why others may disagree with this statement. [6]

Total Marks _____ / 13

Practice Questions

How Can Christians Experience God?

1   What experiences can someone have to make them aware of God?   [2]

2   Name two types of miracle performed by Jesus.   [2]

3   Who receives a vision in Genesis 15:1 and what is revealed?   [2]

4   Describe the nature of the book of Revelation.   [4]

5   How did Jesus show His power over nature in Matthew 14:13–21?   [5]

Total Marks _____ / 15

How Can Life Be Sacred?

1   On what day were humans created and what made this day of creation different than the others?   [2]

2   How are humans separated from the rest of creation?   [2]

3   What is the 'soul'?   [2]

4   How can the sanctity of life be applied to the topic of abortion?   [4]

5   How does the Bible show that life is sacred?   [5]

Total Marks _____ / 15

Practice Questions

Sanctity of Life

1 Why is Genesis 1:27 important? [2]

....

....

2 When do Muslims believe that life begins? [2]

....

....

3 When do the majority of Christians believe that life begins? [4]

....

....

....

....

4 How can religious believers demonstrate their views about when life begins? [5]

....

....

....

....

....

Total Marks .... / 13

Birth Matters

1 Why is Jeremiah 1:5 important to Christians? [2]

....

....

2 Explain the term AIH. [2]

....

....

3 Explain the key religious beliefs about IVF. [4]

....

....

....

....

4 Outline the UK abortion laws. [5]

....

....

....

....

....

Total Marks .... / 13

Marriage and Divorce

1 What is an 'annulment'? [2]

....

....

2 Why are rings exchanged during a marriage? [2]

....

....

3 Why do you think Muslim marriages are often arranged? [2]

....

....

4 Describe four key features of a Jewish marriage. [4]

....

....

....

....

Total Marks .... / 10

Is Family More Important Than Friends?

1. Suggest some of the challenges raised by modern family structures. [2]

2. Why is Ephesians 6:4 important to Christian fathers? [2]

3. Describe the nuclear family. [2]

4. What types of relationships are there? [4]

5. Define the roles within a traditional Christian family. [5]

Total Marks _____ / 15

Are Children the Centre of the Family?

1 What does Psalm 127:3 say about children? [2]

_____

_____

2 What does Jesus say about children in Matthew 19:14? [2]

_____

_____

3 When can a child take the Eucharist in the Catholic Church? [2]

_____

_____

4 How is the importance of children shown in the Church? [4]

_____

_____

_____

_____

5 What key things should happen as part of Christian family life? [5]

_____

_____

_____

_____

_____

Total Marks _____ / 15

Death and Who Can End Life

1 What is 'assisted suicide'? [2]

2 How are active and passive euthanasia different? [2]

3 In which country is the death penalty most frequently carried out and at approximately what rate? [2]

4 Describe the Jewish funeral rites. [4]

5 What typically happens after the death of a Christian? [5]

Total Marks _____ / 15

Can God's Existence Be Argued?

You must be able to:

- Explain the argument for design
- Describe how the existence of the universe can point towards the existence of God
- Evaluate the strengths and weaknesses of both arguments.

The Teleological Argument

- Would anyone look at a watch and presume that it had come into existence by chance?
- Would anyone presume that a rock has come into existence by chance?
- In the 18th century, William Paley argued that the universe around us clearly has a 'design', due to the structure and form that it takes.
- For this to be the case, there had to be a 'designer', an intelligent and thoughtful being – God, who designed this world, and humans, for a purpose.
- As designer, He created a perfect world in sync with itself, much like the mechanism inside a watch.
- The teleological argument did not prove the existence of God, but as science found more evidence for complex structure within every object at an anatomical level, the design argument was strengthened.

> **Key Point**
>
> Many attempts have been made to argue the existence of God, often using the universe and its design as proof for His existence.

The Cosmological Argument

- As understanding of the Earth and the universe changed during the 13th century, St Thomas Aquinas (right) set about using the existence of the universe as proof for God's existence: the cosmological argument.
- The basis for Aquinas' argument is that all things must have been 'caused' and that the universe around us could not have just 'happened'.
- You cannot make something out of nothing.
- He argued that there could not be an infinite number of causes tracing backwards; there must be a 'first cause'.
- He concluded that God was the 'first cause' and put all things into motion.
- He pointed to the expanse of the universe and the intricacies of Earth as proof for his argument.
- Despite scientific understanding changing dramatically (e.g. the Sun being at the centre of the solar system and not the Earth), Aquinas' argument still points to the existence of God without proving it.

Evidence Through Morality

- As we grow up, we become aware of right and wrong.
- However, where do these morals come from?
- Some argue that morality is just something that we are born with or learn and we choose either to accept it or deny it.
- We have a conscience, an 'internal voice', which reminds us how we should behave.
- However, Christians can argue that this sense of morality has to come from somewhere, with God being the obvious source.
- Therefore, human morality points to the existence of God.

Louie Giglio versus Richard Dawkins

- As science and technology advance and develop so do the arguments that rely upon them to either prove or disprove God's existence.
- Louie Giglio (right) and Richard Dawkins (below, right) see themselves adopting polar opposite positions in this debate.
- Theologian Louie Giglio has used the complex structure of the human body and the expanse of the universe to point towards God's existence.
- Focusing on laminin in human skin he builds upon the teleological argument, whereas his use of images from NASA's Hubble telescope reflects the theory of God being proven through the nature of the universe.
- Richard Dawkins has been described as a devout atheist and believes that science now provides us with all the answers that we need.
- In *The God Delusion*, Dawkins states that religion is obsolete and that to believe in the existence of a deity is to deny the truths that science presents.

Points to Consider

- Consider:
  - the statement, 'Atheism requires as much faith as any religion';
  - why, in the face of so many arguments against belief, the vast majority of the world's population still believe;
  - whether belief in God is really dependent on logical argument.

Quick Test

1. What is the cosmological argument based upon?
2. How can a watch compare to a rock?
3. Give reasons to show which of the arguments for the existence of God is most effective.

Key Words

teleological argument
cosmological argument
morality

How Can Beliefs About God Cause Conflict?

You must be able to:

- Describe the most common causes of conflict, including politics, resources, history, culture and religion
- Examine the criteria for a Just War
- Consider recent examples of conflict.

Key Scripture and Religious Teaching

Deuteronomy 7:22–24, 'The LORD your God will drive out those nations before you, little by little … the LORD your God will deliver them over to you, throwing them into great confusion until they are destroyed … No one will be able to stand up against you; you will destroy them.'

Joel 3:9, 'Prepare for war! Rouse the warriors! Let all the fighting men draw near and attack.'

How Does Conflict Start?

- Since the 'fall of man' and fights between Cain and Abel, there has always been conflict.
- Greed, money and power can often be traced as being the catalysts for violence, in addition to political differences and the struggle for natural resources.
- Religious differences can also be a source of conflict for mankind, whether between religions or within the same religion.
- The Old Testament is filled with battles between the Israelites and their enemies, with many victories and defeats for 'God's people'.
- In the New Testament, Jesus commanded the crowd to 'turn the other cheek' when struck, thereby preventing disputes from escalating.

Key Point

War was commonplace in the Old Testament but Jesus' teachings pointed to peace and not to war.

Attitudes to War

- For many Christians, the use of violence should be avoided and a peaceful resolution should be sought. However, some Christians believe there are times when violence may be the only suitable response to stop the spread of evil.
- When considering the use of violence, Christians can turn to the work of St Thomas Aquinas from the 13th century.
- St Thomas Aquinas developed three conditions for a war to be 'just'. These were added to at later dates by other Christians. He called this the Just War Theory.
- A Just War must:
  - have a just cause;
  - be declared by a lawful authority (e.g. a government);
  - have a good intention, with peace being restored afterwards;
  - be a last resort;

- have a reasonable chance of success;
- use proportional force to win;
- bring about more good than the harm that it causes.

Conflict in the Bible

- Throughout the Old Testament books of Deuteronomy, Joshua and Judges, God often told the Israelites to fight and destroy foreign tribes to gain the Promised Land (Israel).
- These accounts of conventional warfare show us that there are times when violence and its use can be justified and even supported by God.
- During His teaching, Jesus made references to violence but placed the emphasis upon peace.
- However, in Matthew 10, verses 34–36, Jesus talks about families being separated and His Word being a sword, not a symbol of peace, indicating that Jesus may support the use of violence.
- However, if the passage is read in context (when the verses before and after are read too), many other Christians argue that the message that Jesus brings is about the division in families (a metaphorical sword dividing families).
- This division would come about because His teachings are different from the Jewish faith and will make members of the same family have to choose which religion to believe in.

Conflict in the 21st Century

- In the last century, the face and nature of war has changed.
- The 20th century saw an acceleration in the development of weaponry with the devastation of the First and Second World Wars.
- Wars in Afghanistan and Iraq have still had an 'on-the-ground' element, but much of the warfare has been conducted from a distance with the use of tactical missiles.
- The move to unconventional warfare has arguably reduced the number of military deaths but has also seen an increase in civilian casualties.
- Christians would argue that the use of nuclear weapons cannot be justified. Weapons of mass destruction are indiscriminate and kill civilians and military alike.
- They would also argue that all weapons designed to kill civilians should be destroyed.

> **Quick Test**
>
> 1. What are the differences between conventional and unconventional warfare?
> 2. In your opinion, what are the main causes of war today?
> 3. List at least four of the Just War criteria.

> **Key Words**
>
> conflict
> **Just War Theory**
> conventional warfare
> **unconventional warfare**

Are There Genuine Alternatives to War?

You must be able to:

- Understand the history of peace in Christianity
- Examine the arguments surrounding pacifism
- Discuss the values of pacifism and conscientious objection.

Key Scripture and Religious Teaching

Proverbs 20:22, 'Do not say, "I'll pay you back for this wrong!" Wait for the LORD, and he will avenge you.'

Matthew 5:9, 'Blessed are the peacemakers, for they will be called children of God.'

Matthew 5:39, 'But I tell you, do not resist an evil person. If anyone slaps you on the right cheek, turn to them the other cheek also.'

To be a Pacifist or a Conscientious Objector?

- Religious believers and secular believers alike have many reasons for objecting to violence.
- If someone is opposed in any way to conflict and violence, then they are a pacifist.
- A conscientious objector is an individual who will refuse to participate in a specific conflict as their conscience will not permit it.
- A pacifist may well be a conscientious objector but that does not mean a conscientious objector is a pacifist.
- For example, a conscientious objector who would not fight or create weapons could be willing to be a medic or prepare food for the army.
- During the Second World War thousands of men and women lost their lives by supporting soldiers as first aid officers, with one of their responsibilities being to try to rescue injured soldiers on the front line.

War and Human Rights

- Protecting human rights at a time of war can be very hard.
- Following the two world wars, in 1948, the United Nations published the Universal Declaration of Human Rights (UDHR), which was designed to protect people at times of war and otherwise (see page 136 for more on the UDHR).

> **Key Point**
>
> An individual can show their opposition to violence by either taking a pacifist view or that of a conscientious objector.

- The Geneva Convention of 1949 set out the rights of civilians during a time of war. It also seeks to protect the rights of prisoners of war and injured soldiers.
- The convention contains 159 articles designed to protect those not active during any conflict.
- The articles relate to issues such as safety and provision during a time of war. They also set out the need for protected medical services and support.

Stop the War Coalition (StWC)

- In recent years, campaigns to raise awareness of war and conflict have been championed through the internet.
- StWC has fought to bring an end to war throughout the world and find ways to influence governments and policies.
- It is a non-political organisation and challenges the use of violence by governments either within their own country or beyond their borders.
- The group is supported by public donations and uses some of these funds to lobby the UK parliament and to encourage it to find alternatives to war.
- StWC believes that diplomacy is the best option and should always be exhausted first.
- Diplomacy is the practice of conducting negotiations between nations in order to find a solution to a problem without causing hostility.

The Dalai Lama

- The 14th Dalai Lama (right) was born in 1935 in the Republic of China (north eastern Tibet).
- In 1940, he was enthroned to his position, which would give him the platform to devote his life to championing peace.
- During the Tibetan uprising, the Dalai Lama escaped from China to India where he continued to live as a refugee.
- As a Buddhist he has sought to spread peace in many countries, including the building of over 200 monasteries.
- In 1989 he was awarded the Nobel Peace Prize and he continued his work thereafter.
- Despite being a Buddhist, his work has been supported by many religious believers, including Christians.

Key Point

Most religious believers would argue that it is better to seek a peaceful resolution than to rely upon violence to solve a dispute.

Quick Test

1. What are the key differences between pacifism and conscientious objection?
2. Describe the work of the Stop the War Coalition.
3. What is stated in the Geneva Convention?

Key Words

pacifist
conscientious objector
UDHR

How are Crimes Punished?

You must be able to:

- Investigate the difference between sin and crime
- Examine the purposes of punishment
- Explore different religious views.

> **Key Scripture and Religious Teaching**

Matthew 5:39, 'But I tell you, do not resist an evil person. If anyone slaps you on the right cheek, turn to them the other cheek also.'

Sins and Crimes

- Many of the laws that govern the UK have their origin in the Ten Commandments given by God to Moses on Mount Sinai (Exodus 20:1–17).
- In religious terms, everyone commits sin but only a few people commit crime.
- A sin is when actions or thoughts contradict the laws of God.
- Crimes are actions against the laws of the country or state.
- However, sins are not always crimes. For example, adultery is clearly a sin for Jews and Christians (Seventh Commandment), but it is not a crime in UK law.
- In the UK, corporal and capital punishment are illegal.
- The last executions in Britain were in August 1964.
- In some countries, there is no distinction between religious law and the law of the state.

The Effects of Crime

- Crimes can occur for a wide variety of reasons. For example, a criminal may be poor and so steals; they may be angry and so cause physical harm; or they may be greedy and so steal to support their lifestyle.
- The effects of a crime can be very far reaching.
- A victim of crime may lose their life or possessions or may suffer physical or psychological harm.
- A victim's family and friends often need support as a result of their loved one's suffering.
- However, the effects of a crime often extend to others not directly related to the victim.
- Society in general suffers because people may feel unsafe as a result of reported crime in the media.
- Insurance premiums can rise and taxes can increase to pay for extra security and the legal system.

> **Key Point**
>
> Crimes may be sins but not all sins are crimes.

The Aims of Punishment

- Forms of punishment include cautions, fines, discharges, community sentences, suspended sentences and imprisonment.
- There are different aims to punishment, influenced by the type of crime committed.
- One of the aims is protection, i.e. preventing the victim and wider society from being harmed by a criminal.
- Some punishments are given as a deterrent in order to discourage others from committing the same offence (e.g. the death penalty for murder).
- Reformation in punishment is designed to help the criminal change their ways, not to reoffend and to support their rehabilitation.
- Reparation requires the offender to try to repair the damage caused by their criminal behaviour and put something back into society. It may involve restorative justice, an approach which gives victims the chance to explain the impact of the crime.
- Retribution is an attempt to make the criminal pay for the crime that they have committed against society.
- Vindication aims to show that offenders must be punished to demonstrate that the law must be respected and is right.
- Most sentences combine different elements of these types of punishment.

Religious Views

- Jesus was faced with many questions about sin, crime and punishment.
- His response was focused on the application of what He taught were the two greatest commandments: loving God and loving your neighbour as yourself (Matthew 22:37–39).
- Jesus was teaching that all actions should be out of love for another person.
- When asked about paying taxes to Caesar (Matthew 22:15–22), Jesus' reply suggests that you should obey the law of the land but also, and ultimately more importantly, obey God's commands.
- For Christians, the teaching in the New Testament is very different to that in the Old Testament.
- Jewish justice was largely based on retribution: 'Eye for an eye, tooth for a tooth. As he has injured the others so he is to be injured.' (Leviticus 24:19–20).
- Islamic countries that practise Sharia law allow capital punishment for two types of crime:
  - intentional murder;
  - threatening to undermine authority or destabilise the state.
- There is a debate in the UK about Muslims holding their own courts of justice based on Sharia law.

> **Key Point**
>
> Protection, deterrence, reformation, reparation, retribution and vindication are the main aims of punishment.

> **Key Words**
>
> sin
> crime
> corporal punishment
> deterrent
> reformation
> reparation
> restorative justice
> retribution
> vindication

> **Quick Test**
>
> 1. List the main reasons for punishment.
> 2. How is society damaged by crime?
> 3. What is 'capital punishment'?

Poverty and Wealth

You must be able to:

- Describe different degrees of, the causes of and the consequences of poverty
- Explain what is being done to try to ease poverty
- Discuss attitudes towards, the uses of and the responsibilities of wealth.

Key Scripture and Religious Teaching

Deuteronomy 15:7–8, 'At the end of every seven years...every creditor shall release what he has lent to his neighbour...'

Timothy 6: 10, 'For the love of money is the root of all evil: which while some coveted after, they have erred from the faith, and pierced themselves through with many sorrows.'

Matthew 6:19, 'Do not store up riches for yourself here on earth. Instead store up riches in heaven.'

Different Degrees of Poverty

- What is deemed as poverty in one location can be far different from what is considered poverty in another.
- Someone living in poverty in the UK may well have a roof over their heads and have clothes in their wardrobe but may have to make decisions as to how to divide their money between paying heating bills and buying food.
- Another person living in Sierra Leone may be living in poverty but only have the clothes that they stand in, no home and may not know where their next meal is coming from.

Key Point

Poverty is relative to the place in which people live.

Causes of Poverty

- The divide between the poverty of the developing world and the wealth of the Western world can be attributed to human greed and exploitation.
- Throughout history, much of Africa has seen its resources used and sold by richer countries and the money taken away.
- It is now widely understood that 20% of the world's population controls 80% of the world's wealth. This has led to developing countries incurring heavy debts and millions of people being unable to access basic needs such as food and water.
- Natural disasters can also force people into poverty. For example, hurricanes, earthquakes and floods in Haiti have killed many thousands of people over the last 10 years alone, destroying homes and other buildings in the process.

Key Point

There are many causes of poverty, some of which are caused by humans and others which are not.

Consequences of Poverty

- Many lives are lost as a result of a lack of food, inadequate sanitation, poor medical provision and people being forced to live in vulnerable conditions.

- For example, large areas of Bangladesh are at sea level and are used by many to grow rice to live off. However, high tides and heavy rain often leave much of this land flooded, with people losing their homes, food and even their lives.
- People trying to escape poverty can lead to them being exploited by criminal gangs, unscrupulous employers and loan sharks.
- The human-trafficking industry takes advantage of men, women and children seeking a better life for themselves and their families.
- Victims can find themselves kidnapped into slavery or forced prostitution with little hope of escape.
- In both developing and developed countries, migrant workers have been exploited in so-called 'sweatshops', enduring dangerous conditions, abuse, excessive overtime, denial of rights and poor pay.
- Meanwhile, money lenders have been accused of exploiting low-income borrowers with excessively high interest rates and hidden fees, thereby trapping them in a cycle of debt.

Tackling Poverty

- Every religion teaches its followers to help those around them, and this includes the poor.
- Some believers may buy fair trade goods to ensure that the poor receive as much money as possible for their products and to help improve their lives.
- Many others will support the work of charities which strive to help people rise out of poverty and campaign for global justice.
- Such organisations include Christian Aid, Tearfund, the Catholic Agency For Overseas Development (CAFOD), Muslim Aid, Islamic Relief and World Jewish Relief.
- Jews and Christians have specific teachings about debt, one of the main causes of poverty.
- Deuteronomy 15: 7–8 shows that those in debt should not have it held over them, forcing them into poverty, and instead should be given the opportunity to be freed from their debts.
- In 2000, the Jubilee 2000 appeal set out to raise awareness of poverty in the developing world and prompt wealthier governments to cancel the debt owed to them by poorer countries. This did make a difference but thousands continue to die across the world each day.

> **Key Point**
>
> Make sure you are familiar with the work of some of the charities working to relieve poverty and suffering.

Is it Wrong to be Rich?

- If a religious believer should always help those who have less than them, it could be argued that it would be wrong for a believer to be rich.
- However, Timothy 6:10 does not say that money is the root of all evil but the love of it is, as this would make a person greedy and selfish.
- In Matthew 6:19, Jesus also taught that Christians should think about the afterlife when they think about possessions and money.

> **Quick Test**
>
> 1. What is 'poverty'?
> 2. Name a charity working to help fight poverty.
> 3. What are 'natural disasters'?

> **Key Word**
>
> poverty
> wealth
> exploitation

Is Everyone Truly Equal?

You must be able to:

- Explain and give examples of prejudice and discrimination
- Understand the equality of men and women shown in Christianity and the Bible and the different attitudes shown to women in Genesis compared to the New Testament
- Describe the nature of discrimination and how it has been challenged.

Key Scripture and Religious Teaching

Luke 10:27, 'Love your neighbour as you love yourself'.

Luke 10:25–37, The Good Samaritan

Galatians 3:28, 'There is neither Jew nor Gentile, neither slave nor free, nor is there male and female, for you are all one in Christ Jesus.'

What is the Difference Between Prejudice and Discrimination?

- **Prejudice** is the term given to thoughts based on pre-conceived ideas that often create negative stereotypes of groups of people.
- **Discrimination** is when prejudiced thoughts are acted upon.

How People are Treated Differently

- Racism has seen millions of people treated differently because of the colour of their skin or because of their country of origin, e.g. apartheid in South Africa.
- Sexism has seen men and women divided throughout history, with women often being seen as lesser than men.
- Poverty is a big cause of discrimination, with people treated badly because they have less money or come from a poorer background.
- Another notable prejudice exists towards people who have either physical disabilities or learning difficulties.
- Homophobia and sexual orientation have become big issues in recent decades, with both men and women victimised because of their sexuality.

Key Point

Humans often judge one another on grounds such as skin colour, gender and sexual orientation.

Who Has Stood Against Discrimination?

- Martin Luther King Jr was instrumental in the ending of separation between whites and blacks in the USA.
- The bus system was an example of segregation in the USA, with black people being forced to give up their seats for white people.
- In 1955 Rosa Parks, a 42-year-old black lady, refused to give up her seat on a bus. This led to a boycotting of the bus system by the black community.
- King strived for equality, endorsing only non-violent protest and in 1963 gave his 'I have a dream' speech, leading to him being awarded the Nobel Peace Prize, before being assassinated in 1968.
- Born in 1910, Mother Teresa fought to overcome the issue of poverty over a period of 45 years, working with the poor and sick in Calcutta, India.
- She showed the world that all people should be treated equally regardless of their background and that those with more should help those with less.
- In 1979 Mother Teresa was also awarded the Nobel Peace Prize and then, in 1980, the Bharat Ratna, India's highest civilian honour.

Is Christianity Discriminatory?

- The world's major religions teach the principle of the 'Golden Rule': each person should behave in a way in which they would expect to be treated.
- However, it has only been in recent years that women have begun to gain equal rights to men in Christianity.
- Throughout the Old Testament, almost all of the key figures were male, with God revealing Himself through male prophets.
- In the New Testament, Paul writes in numerous letters about how women are still separated from men.
- During the 20th century many areas of the Church have looked to close the gap between men and women.
- In some denominations, churches have appointed female priests and bishops, providing men and women with equal opportunities to hold positions of authority in the Church.

Key Point

Jesus taught that all should be treated equally, regardless of their differences.

Quick Test

1. How has the Church's attitude changed towards women?
2. List reasons given for treating people differently.
3. Explain the principle behind the Good Samaritan story.

Key Words

prejudice
discrimination
apartheid
Golden Rule

What Does it Mean to Have Human Rights?

You must be able to:

- Explore what is meant by 'human rights'
- Investigate the practical promotion of human rights
- Explain how UK law tries to protect people.

Key Scripture and Religious Teaching

Luke 10:27, 'Jesus said, "Love your neighbour as you love yourself".'

What are Human Rights?

- Human rights are ideals that describe standards of human behaviour and are protected as legal rights in law.
- These rights can be described as inalienable, which means a person is entitled to them simply because they are human, regardless of their nation, location, language, religion or ethnic origin.
- They are universal rights and are the same for everyone.
- They impose an obligation on individuals to respect the human rights of others.
- Human rights should not be taken away, except as a result of due legal process (for example, if someone is sent to prison).

Key Point

All human beings are entitled to a minimum standard of treatment.

Universal Declaration of Human Rights (UDHR)

- During times of war it is often difficult to protect the rights of individuals, whether they are soldiers or civilians.
- In 1947, the Human Rights Commission began to discuss an International Bill of Rights, partly as a response to the atrocities of the Second World War.
- In 1948 the United Nations convened to create the Universal Declaration of Human Rights (UDHR).
- The declaration set out 30 'articles' to ensure that individuals were protected from harm under law, including:
  - right to life;
  - freedom from torture;
  - freedom from slavery;
  - right to a fair trial.
- All UN nations agreed to these articles and agreed to support their implementation.
- The articles protect basic human rights and aim to stop persecution, whilst allowing freedom of movement and speech.

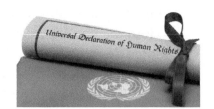

Key Point

Minimum standards of treatment are contained in the UDHR.

Amnesty International

- In 1961 British lawyer Peter Benenson founded Amnesty International as a pacifist organisation after he read about social injustice in Portugal.
- It is a global movement of more than 7 million people who campaign to end abuses of human rights, including demanding justice for those whose rights have been violated.
- Amnesty International's work has focused on seeing the UDHR upheld around the world and finding new ways to protect the rights of humanity.
- This has often centred on those mistreated by their government, with particular efforts made to aid the release of those falsely imprisoned.
- Much of Amnesty International's work takes place during times of war but is not limited to those periods.
- The organisation is committed to:
  - freeing prisoners of conscience;
  - gaining a fair trial for political prisoners;
  - ending torture, political killings and 'disappearances';
  - abolishing the death penalty throughout the world.
- In 1977, Amnesty International was awarded the Nobel Peace Prize and, in 1978, the United Nations Human Rights Prize.

The UK Human Rights Act

- The UK Human Rights Act of 1998 sought to incorporate into UK law the rights contained in the European Convention on Human Rights.
- The Act makes it unlawful for UK public bodies to act in ways that are incompatible with the Convention.
- It also requires the courts to take account of any decisions made by the European Court of Human Rights.
- Courts must also interpret legislation in a way that is compatible with the Convention.
- This legislation is often revisited as changes in technology and science create new situations, such as data protection and its restricted use, which might infringe human rights.

Quick Test

1. What is the purpose of the Universal Declaration of Human Rights?
2. Outline the work of Amnesty International.
3. When did Amnesty International receive the Nobel Peace Prize?
4. Why is the UK Human Rights Act important for Britain?

Key Words

inalienable
universal

Review Questions

How Can Christians Experience God?

1 Why are visions important in religion? [1]

2 What event took place in Matthew 8:23–27? [1]

3 How can near-death experiences help religious believers even if they do not experience them themselves? [4]

4 'Miracles that are recorded in the Bible no longer happen, which suggests that they were not real.'

Explain three reasons why some may agree with this statement and three reasons why others may disagree with this statement. [6]

Total Marks _____ / 12

How Can Life Be Sacred?

1 What is abortion? [1]

....

2 Outline what is meant by the 'sanctity of life'. [2]

....

....

3 Explain why you think John 3:16 is significant for Christians. [4]

....

....

....

....

4 'There should be no need for active euthanasia in the UK because of the strength of the hospice movement.'

Explain three reasons why some may agree with this statement and three reasons why others may disagree with this statement. [6]

....

....

....

....

....

....

Total Marks .... / 13

Review Questions

Sanctity of Life

1 Define the term 'ruh'. [1]

2 At what stage do Jews generally believe that life has been fully granted by God during pregnancy? [1]

3 What happens at conception? [1]

4 'Religious attitudes to when life begins are less important than what UK law states.'

Explain three reasons why some may agree with this statement and three reasons why others may disagree with this statement. [6]

Total Marks _____ / 9

Birth Matters

1 What does the abbreviation IVF stand for? [1]

....

2 At what stage can a pregnancy be terminated in the UK? [1]

....

3 Explain the process of IVF. [4]

....

....

....

....

4 'The morning after pill is a form of abortion.'

Explain three reasons why some may agree with this statement and three reasons why others may disagree with this statement. [6]

....

....

....

....

....

....

Total Marks .... / 12

Review Questions

Marriage and Divorce

1 In a Sikh marriage ceremony, why do the couple bow before the Guru Granth Sahib? [2]

....

....

2 Explain the main reasons why Christians get married. [4]

....

....

....

....

3 'If a Christian feels they have to divorce, they should not want to remarry.'

Explain three reasons why some may agree with this statement and three reasons why others may disagree with this statement. [6]

....

....

....

....

....

Total Marks .... / 12

Is Family More Important Than Friends?

1 What is the Fifth Commandment? [1]

2 What does Paul argue for in Galatians 3:28? [1]

3 What is a 'blended family'? [1]

4 Explain how the traditional roles of husbands and wives have changed. [4]

5 'The best place for children to be brought up is within marriage.'

Explain three reasons why some may agree with this statement and three reasons why others may disagree with this statement. [6]

Total Marks .... / 13

Are Children the Centre of the Family?

1 What is an alternative to infant baptism? [1]

2 What festival is used to remind Christians about the resurrection of Jesus? [1]

3 As a family, how can parents help the spiritual development of their children? [1]

4 Why do you think some Christians choose dedication over infant baptism? [4]

5 'All young Christians should go through the passage of confirmation.'

Explain three reasons why some may agree with this statement and three reasons why others may disagree with this statement. [6]

Total Marks _____ / 13

Death and Who Can End Life

1 What is 'euthanasia'? [1]

....

2 What happens to the body of a Muslim after they die? [1]

....

3 Why do you think many religious believers disagree with the death penalty? [2]

....

....

4 Explain the importance of Job 1:21 in discussions about euthanasia. [4]

....

....

....

....

5 'The death penalty is the most appropriate punishment for murder.'

Explain three reasons why some may agree with this statement and three reasons why
others may disagree with this statement. [6]

....

....

....

....

....

Total Marks .... / 14

Can God's Existence Be Argued?

1. Name two arguments for the existence of God. [2]

2. Who is Louie Giglio? [2]

3. Who is Richard Dawkins? [2]

4. How can morality suggest God's existence? [4]

5. How did William Paley argue for the existence of God? [5]

Total Marks _____ / 15

How Can Beliefs About God Cause Conflict?

1. What are two of the main causes of conflict? [2]

2. Where is the first incident of violence recorded in the Bible?
What was the cause of the conflict? [2]

3. What two commands were given to the Jews in Joel 3:9? [2]

4. What did Jesus teach about conflict? [4]

5. Describe the work of St Thomas Aquinas on the theme of war. [5]

Total Marks _____ / 15

Are There Genuine Alternatives to War?

1 What was written in 1948 and what was its aim? [2]

2 Who is the Dalai Lama? [2]

3 Which group of people are mentioned in Matthew 5:9 and how are they described? [2]

4 What views might Christians take when they oppose war? [4]

5 Describe the work of the Stop the War Coalition. [5]

Total Marks .... / 15

How are Crimes Punished?

1 Define 'corporal punishment' and give an example. [2]

2 Give two alternatives to custodial punishments. [2]

3 What are key UK laws based upon and where are they found in the Bible? [2]

4 What are four of the aims of punishment? [4]

5 How can crime affect people? [5]

Total Marks _____ / 15

Poverty and Wealth

1. State two ways in which poverty in the UK could be regarded as different to poverty in the developing world. [2]

2. List two ways in which poverty could be eased. [2]

3. In Matthew 19, Jesus teaches that it is harder for a rich man to enter heaven than it is for a camel to enter through the eye of a needle. What do you think this means? [2]

4. Evaluate whether money brings about more good than bad. [4]

5. Describe some of the ways in which poverty can make people vulnerable to exploitation, giving examples. [5]

Total Marks _____ / 15

Is Everyone Truly Equal?

1. How are prejudice and discrimination different? [2]

2. Who was Martin Luther King Jr? [2]

3. What was apartheid? [2]

4. State four common types of prejudice. [4]

5. What did Jesus teach through the parable of the Good Samaritan? [5]

Total Marks _____ / 15

Practice Questions

What Does it Mean to Have Human Rights?

1 What are 'human rights'? [2]

_____

_____

2 What events led to the writing of the UDHR? [2]

_____

_____

3 When was the UDHR written and how many articles does it include? [2]

_____

_____

4 List four of the basic human rights set out in the UDHR. [4]

_____

_____

_____

_____

5 How are the UDHR and the Human Rights Act different? [5]

_____

_____

_____

_____

_____

Total Marks _____ / 15

Can God's Existence Be Argued?

1 Define 'morality'. [1]

2 In what book does Richard Dawkins argue against the existence of God? [1]

3 Name the argument that is based upon design. [1]

4 Describe the argument for the existence of God as laid out by St Thomas Aquinas. [4]

5 'Science will never be able to remove the need for religion in humanity.'

Explain three reasons why some may agree with this statement and three reasons why others may disagree with this statement. [6]

Total Marks _____ / 13

How Can Beliefs About God Cause Conflict?

1 Name one scholar who helped develop the Just War Theory. [1]

2 What is a weapon of mass destruction? [1]

3 In what passage are the Jews called to be ready for war? [1]

4 Explain the difference between war and conflict. [4]

5 'No war can ever be justified due to the inevitable loss of innocent life.'

Explain three reasons why some may agree with this statement and three reasons why others may disagree with this statement. [6]

Total Marks _____ / 13

Are There Genuine Alternatives to War?

1 Define the term 'pacifist'. [1]

2 Define the term 'conscientious objector'. [1]

3 What is the role of diplomacy during conflict? [1]

4 Describe what can be done to prevent war. [4]

5 'A Christian should never opt to fight during a time of war.'

Explain three reasons why some may agree with this statement and three reasons why others may disagree with this statement. [6]

Total Marks _____ / 13

How are Crimes Punished?

1 What crime carries the greatest possible prison sentence in the UK? [1]

....

2 What is a 'sin'? [1]

....

3 What aim of punishment focuses on the recovery of the criminal? [1]

....

4 State some of the ways in which a criminal can be punished in the UK. [4]

....

....

....

....

5 'All punishments should ensure that provision is made to help the criminal not to reoffend in the future.'

Explain three reasons why some may agree with this statement and three reasons why others may disagree with this statement. [6]

....

....

....

....

....

....

Total Marks .... / 13

Poverty and Wealth

1 Name two types of natural disaster. [1]

2 Give two ways in which someone might get into debt. [2]

3 What did the Jubilee 2000 appeal aim to do? [2]

4 Explain why a religious believer may support a charity that cares for the poor. [3]

5 'Mankind will never be able to eliminate poverty.'

Explain three reasons why some may agree with this statement and three reasons why others may disagree with this statement. [6]

Total Marks .... / 14

Review Questions

Is Everyone Truly Equal?

1 What term is given to discrimination based upon age? [1]

2 Define the 'Golden Rule'. [1]

3 Explain how a government can work to reduce prejudice. [4]

4 'All religious believers should work to treat all people equally.'

Explain three reasons why some may agree with this statement and three reasons why others may disagree with this statement. [6]

Total Marks _____ / 12

What Does it Mean to Have Human Rights?

1 Name a leading world charity that works to support the victims of injustice. [1]

2 Which countries signed up to the UDHR? [1]

3 Who was the founder of Amnesty International? [1]

4 How is Luke 10:27 central to Christian beliefs about human rights? [4]

5 'As humanity suffers from the grip of greed, the people of the world will never receive all of their human rights.'

Explain three reasons why some may agree with this statement and three reasons why others may disagree with this statement. [6]

Total Marks .... / 13

Creation

Source A

Genesis 1

New International Version

The Beginning

[1]In the beginning God created the heavens and the earth. [2]Now the earth was formless and empty, darkness was over the surface of the deep, and the Spirit of God was hovering over the waters.

[3]And God said, "Let there be light," and there was light. [4]God saw that the light was good, and he separated the light from the darkness. [5]God called the light "day", and the darkness he called "night". And there was evening, and there was morning—the first day.

[6]And God said, "Let there be a vault between the waters to separate water from water." [7]So God made the vault and separated the water under the vault from the water above it. And it was so. [8]God called the vault "sky". And there was evening, and there was morning—the second day.

[9]And God said, "Let the water under the sky be gathered to one place, and let dry ground appear." And it was so. [10]God called the dry ground "land", and the gathered waters he called "seas". And God saw that it was good.

[11]Then God said, "Let the land produce vegetation: seed-bearing plants and trees on the land that bear fruit with seed in it, according to their various kinds." And it was so. [12]The land produced vegetation: plants bearing seed according to their kinds and trees bearing fruit with seed in it according to their kinds. And God saw that it was good. [13]And there was evening, and there was morning—the third day.

[14]And God said, "Let there be lights in the vault of the sky to separate the day from the night, and let them serve as signs to mark sacred times, and days and years, [15]and let them be lights in the vault of the sky to give light on the earth." And it was so. [16]God made two great lights—the greater light to govern the day and the lesser light to govern the night. He also made the stars. [17]God set them in the vault of the sky to give light on the earth, [18]to govern the day and the night, and to separate light from darkness. And God saw that it was good. [19]And there was evening, and there was morning—the fourth day.

[20]And God said, "Let the water teem with living creatures, and let birds fly above the earth across the vault of the sky." [21]So God created the great creatures of the sea and every living thing with which the water teems and that moves about in it, according to their kinds, and every winged bird according to its kind. And God saw that it was good. [22]God blessed them and said, "Be fruitful and increase in number and fill the water in the seas, and let the birds increase on the earth." [23]And there was evening, and there was morning—the fifth day.

[24]And God said, "Let the land produce living creatures according to their kinds: the livestock, the creatures that move along the ground, and the wild animals, each according to its kind." And it was so. [25]God made the wild animals according to their kinds, the livestock according to their kinds, and all the creatures that move along the ground according to their kinds. And God saw that it was good.

[26]Then God said, "Let us make mankind in our image, in our likeness, so that they may rule over the fish in the sea and the birds in the sky, over the livestock and all the wild animals, and over all the creatures that move along the ground."

[27]So God created mankind in his own image,

in the image of God he created them;

male and female he created them.

28God blessed them and said to them, "Be fruitful and increase in number; fill the earth and subdue it. Rule over the fish in the sea and the birds in the sky and over every living creature that moves on the ground."

29Then God said, "I give you every seed-bearing plant on the face of the whole earth and every tree that has fruit with seed in it. They will be yours for food. 30And to all the beasts of the earth and all the birds in the sky and all the creatures that move along the ground—everything that has the breath of life in it—I give every green plant for food." And it was so.

31God saw all that he had made, and it was very good. And there was evening, and there was morning—the sixth day.

1 Do you think that this account is physically possible? [4]

....

....

....

....

2 How has scientific knowledge argued against this account? [3]

....

....

....

3 Why do you think that Christian and Islamic views on creation are so similar? [3]

....

....

....

4 How might a Christian respond to the lack of dinosaurs in this account? [2]

....

....

Total Marks .... / 12

Mixed Questions

Prejudice

Source A

1. What issues does this image make you think about? [2]

_____

_____

2. How might Christianity appear to promote discrimination? [4]

_____

_____

_____

_____

3. How could less discrimination lead to less conflict? [3]

_____

_____

_____

4. Why might a pacifist group use a picture like this in its publications? [3]

_____

_____

_____

Total Marks _____ / 12

Ten Commandments

Source A

1. Describe the events and the subsequent episodes surrounding the giving of the
Ten Commandments. **[3]**

2. Why do you think the Ten Commandments were important for the nomadic Hebrews? **[4]**

3. Which of the Ten Commandments can be detected in UK law? **[3]**

4. Select one of the Ten Commandments that you think is still relevant and explain why. **[2]**

Total Marks .... / 12

Mixed Questions

The Elderly

Source A

1 What issues for the elderly might this image suggest? [4]

_____

_____

_____

_____

2 What is the hospice movement and how does it work? [3]

_____

_____

_____

3 What are the main views about euthanasia? [3]

_____

_____

_____

4 Why do some people fear getting old? [2]

_____

_____

Total Marks _____ / 12

Marriage

Source A: Church of England wedding vows

At the point when the vows are said, you turn to each other, take each other's right hand and say:

'I, (name), take you, (name)
to be my wife/husband,
to have and to hold
from this day forward;
for better, for worse,
for richer, for poorer,
in sickness and in health,
to love and to cherish,
till death us do part,
according to God's holy law.
In the presence of God I make this vow.'

1. List four reasons why people might choose a church wedding. [4]

2. What issues might be raised by the bride wearing white? [3]

3. List three elements that are common in marriage services (rites) in different religions. [3]

4. Having made the vows listed above, why might divorce be an issue for those making them? [2]

Total Marks _____ / 12

Punishment

Source A

1 The electric chair is a form of capital punishment. What are the issues associated with its use? [4]

2 What are the main purposes of punishing criminals? [3]

3 What is the difference between a crime and a sin? [3]

4 What is the status of capital punishment in the UK? [2]

Total Marks .... / 12

Death and After

Source A

1 What evidence is there for life after death? [3]

2 What do different faiths believe happens after death? [6]

3 How do Muslims mark the end of life? [3]

Total Marks _____ / 12

Mixed Questions

Worship

1 Why do people worship? [3]

....

....

....

2 What are the main elements of collective worship? [4]

....

....

....

....

3 Why are bread and wine special for Christians? [3]

....

....

....

....

4 Name the special buildings for worship in different faiths. [2]

....

....

Total Marks .... / 12

Answers

Note: You may be able to offer other suitable responses not listed in these Answers

Pages 4–13 **Review Questions**

Pages 4–7
1. Bethlehem [1]
2. Nazareth [1]
3. Mary and Joseph [1]
4. Shepherds and wise men [1]
5. Gold [1]; frankincense [1]; myrrh [1]
6. John the Baptist [1]
7. River Jordan [1]
8. The Holy Spirit came upon him in the form of a dove; 'You are my son…' [1]
9. 40 days and nights [1]
10. **Any one from:** Stones to bread; jump off Temple; worship Satan [1]
11. 12 [1]
12. The rock or stone [1]
13. Anointed one [1]
14. Story with a hidden meaning [1]
15. Turn the other cheek [1]
16. Eternity with God [1]
17. As you would like them to treat you [1]
18. Event that cannot be explained by natural causes [1]
19. **Any one from:** healing; nature; resurrections [1]
20. **Any three from:** Bread and wine; body and blood of Jesus; predicts betrayal; washes disciples' feet; predicts denial [3]
21. In the 'upper room' [1]
22. Judas Iscariot [1]
23. Crucifixion [1]
24. Two criminals [1]
25. In Joseph of Arimathea's tomb [1]
26. When God miraculously brought Jesus back to life [1]
27. Women who came to anoint the body [1]
28. Father [1]
29. Church [1]
30. Where the sermon is preached [1]
31. Where the Bible is read [1]
32. A receptacle for the water used in baptism [1]
33. Where communion is served [1]
34. The Bible [1]
35. Old Testament and New Testament [1]
36. Prayer is communication with God [1]; adoration, confession, thanksgiving and supplication are the main forms of prayer [1]; Christians pray together and in private [1]
37. Sing hymns; say prayers; read scriptures; listen to sermons [1]
38. They believe God speaks to them through the Bible [1]
39. **Any five from:** In baptism, names are given; prayers are said; promises are made; water is sprinkled on the head; sign of the cross is made on the head; lit candle is given [5]
40. **Any three from:** Prayers are said; scriptures read; memories shared; burial or cremation [3]

Pages 8–9
1. Muhammad [1]
2. 570–632 AD [1]
3. Khadija [1]
4. Angel Jibril (Gabriel) [1]
5. Teachings given to Muhammad [1]
6. 622 AD [1]
7. Mecca (Makkah) [1]
8. Allah [1]
9. Mosque [1]
10. Midday Friday [1]
11. Remove shoes [1]; may cover heads [1]; ritual washing (wudu) [1]
12. A tower for the call to prayer [1]
13. Qur'an [1]
14. Arabic [1]
15. **Any four from:** Muslims pray five times a day; they face Mecca; before prayer they ritually wash (wudu); they use a prayer mat when not in the mosque; rak'ah are ritual movements in prayer [4]
16. **Any one from:** Say prayers; read scriptures; listen to sermons; carrying out Five Pillars of Islam [1]
17. Guides their life [1]
18. **Any four from:** Call to prayer whispered in baby's ears; soft part of date on baby's lips; head shaved – silver given to charity – hair buried; circumcision; ritual slaughtering of sheep [4]

Pages 10–11
1. Abraham [1]
2. Moses [1]
3. Jews left Egypt after 10 plagues [1]
4. Crossed the Red Sea [1]
5. Mount Sinai [1]
6. Tablets of stone [1]
7. Yahweh [1]
8. Synagogue [1]
9. Sabbath (Friday evening to Saturday evening) [1]
10. In the Ark [1]
11. Podium where the scriptures are read [1]
12. The eternal light [1]
13. Minimum number of men to allow worship [1]; 10 adult male Jews [1]
14. Tenakh (Tanakh) [1]
15. Hebrew [1]
16. **Any three from:** Pray singly, as a family and as a congregation; three times a day – morning, afternoon, evening; siddur (prayer book) is used; thanksgiving, praise and petition [3]
17. **Any three from:** Sing hymns; say prayers; read from the Law and the Prophets; listen to sermon [3]
18. **Any four from:** Brit Milah – boys are circumcised after eight days; the mohel is a trained circumciser; name given (everyday and religious names); prayers said; girls receive name during next reading of Torah [4]

Pages 12–13
1. Nanak [1]
2. 1469–1539 AD [1]
3. Gobind Singh [1]
4. 1666–1708 AD [1]
5. The Sikh brotherhood [1]
6. Five [1]
7. Ten [1]
8. Kesh – uncut hair [1]; Kanga – comb [1]; Kara – steel bracelet [1]; Kaccha – practical shorts [1]; Kirpan – ritual sword [1]
9. Gurdwara [1]
10. Any day – mainly Sunday in the West [1]
11. Raised platform [1]
12. A person who reads the scripture [1]
13. Ritual pudding [1]
14. Guru Granth Sahib [1]
15. **Any four from:** Bow before Granth; sing hymns; say prayers; read scriptures; ritual meal; service (Sewa) [4]
16. Words spoken by Gurus from God (Waheguru) [1]
17. **Any three from:** Naam Karan in Gurdwara; joyful hymns; Kara Parshad; gifts to Granth; Amrit given to mother and baby; first letter of name from hymn on random page of Guru Granth Sahib [3]

Pages 14–29 **Revise Questions**

Page 15 Quick Test
1. One God existing in three 'persons'; the triune God
2. The Father, the Son and the Holy Spirit
3. The Creator
4. Salvation
5. Continues the Father's work and sanctifies

Page 17 Quick Test
1. Greeks: the creative force, as well as logic and reason; Jews: the way in which God communicated with His people
2. The 'Word' became flesh; virgin birth; immaculate conception
3. He spent 40 days and 40 nights in the desert being tempted
4. Healing miracles; nature miracles; resurrection miracles
5. The tomb was found to be empty; the body was gone; followers were told that Jesus had been raised

Page 19 Quick Test
1. Cremation is forbidden for Jews and Muslims; Sikhs have to be cremated; Christians can be cremated or buried
2. Sikhs believe that the soul enters a new body and the status of the new life is dictated by the quality of the old life

Page 21 Quick Test
1. An in-between state of cleansing and preparation for heaven
2. Some believe based on their actions, others on if they have accepted Jesus' gift of salvation.

Page 23 Quick Test
1. Adam and Eve disobeyed God by eating the forbidden fruit
2. It would take away our free will
3. Because they either deny the existence of God, or are selfish in their actions

Page 25 Quick Test
1. Water is poured on the baby's head, symbolising cleansing and rebirth
2. It reaffirms the baptismal vows and enables the person to take responsibility for their own faith
3. The belief that the bread and wine change into the body and blood of Christ (some Catholics believe that the bread and wine represent the blood and body of Christ, but do not actually change)
4. It contributes to the mission of the Church through the birth and upbringing of children and confers on them the grace they need

Page 27 Quick Test
1. Seek guidance; show gratitude; intercession; adoration; forgiveness; closer to God
2. Lord's Prayer (Our Father)
3. Jewish prayer book
4. Close eyes; kneel; bow head; face mihrab; rak'ah; cover head with tallit

Page 29 Quick Test

1. As a penance; for healing; out of devotion; to honour God
2. To visit holy sites relating to Christianity and Judaism
3. The waters are thought to bring healing; a vision of Mary
4. Pilgrimage to Mecca (Makkah)
5. Pray

Page 30

1. The belief that God is one being with three forms [1]; the Trinity is made up of God the Father, God the Son (Jesus) and God the Holy Spirit. [1]
2. God existed before the universe was created [1]; God the Father created the universe in six days. [1]
3. **Any three from:** Jesus; Christ; Messiah; Saviour; Lord; Emmanuel; Son of Man; Master [2] [1 mark for two]
4. **Any four from:** Deuteronomy 6:4; 1 Corinthians 8:4; John 14:16–17; 1 Corinthians 8:6; Ephesians 3:5 [4]
5. **Any five from:** It helps them to recognise the different characteristics of each member of the Trinity [1], to help shape their relationships with them [1]; God the Father brought them into existence, Jesus sacrificed himself for them [1] and the Holy Spirit works with them on earth [1]; the concept of the Trinity can be confusing and could be seen as a contradiction of the Christian belief of one God [1]; personification can distract from the holiness of God [1]

Page 31

1. His birth and name were proclaimed by angels [1]; His was an immaculate conception to the Virgin Mary [1]
2. The Magi (the Wise Men) [1] and the shepherds [1]
3. Baptised by John the Baptist in the River Jordan [1]; spent 40 days and nights in the desert while being tempted by Satan [1]
4. For Christians, Jesus' death was part of a divine plan to save humanity [1]; He gave His life as a ransom [1]; redeeming believers from the effects of their sins [1]; and restoring people's relationship with God [1]
5. Jesus fulfilled the prophecies of the Old Testament [1]; He submitted to the will of His Father, not resisting His responsibility [1]; the belief that Jesus is the Messiah created the separation from Judaism [1]; the resurrection hailed the start of Christianity and showed God's power over death [1]; Jesus' sacrifice allowed forgiveness for all sins and opened heaven to those who followed Christ [1]

Page 32

1. Heaven, hell or purgatory [2] [1 mark for two]
2. Family member of the same gender washes and wraps the body soon after death [1]; the grave is dug parallel to Mecca [1]
3. Washed in yogurt [1] and dressed in the Five Ks [1]
4. **Any four from:** Life either moves through a cycle or along a ladder; karma throughout someone's life dictates their position in the next life; good karma helps a life move towards spiritual enlightenment; bad karma can see a life regress in the cycle or down the ladder of life; complete spiritual enlightenment sees the mortal life end and the spirit leave the physical world [4]
5. Genesis 1:1 – 'God created the heavens and the earth' [1]; there are a further 20 references to heaven in the book of Genesis alone, 622 in total in the entirety of the Bible [1]; Matthew 3:2 – 'Repent, for the kingdom of heaven has come near' [1]; Matthew 28:2 – 'There was a violent earthquake, for an angel of the Lord came down from heaven and, going to the tomb, rolled back the stone and sat on it' [1]; the book of Revelation reveals the end of the world and the nature of heaven and hell to come [1]

Page 33

1. Heaven or hell [1]
2. Near-death experiences [1]; an event where someone believes they leave their body when close to death or have died [1]
3. God sent Jesus to save the sins of the world as He loved the world [1]; anyone who accepts Jesus as Lord and Saviour has the hope of this resurrection life with God. [1]
4. **Any four from:** The soul lives on after death to be judged; God's judgement confines the soul to either heaven or hell; the body is raised and transformed, to live on in heaven or hell; in addition, some Catholics believe the soul may be sent to purgatory; purgatory is a place for those not yet ready for heaven. [4]
5. Allah will judge Muslims on the decisions that they make [1]; all will be judged on the Day of Resurrection [1]; Jannah (paradise) is set apart for those who have pleased Allah [1]; Jahannam (hell) is the eternal destination for those who fail Allah's judgement [1]; Allah is merciful and will forgive sins, except for those who deny Him. [1]

Page 34

1. The defence of God in response to the problem of evil [1]; how can an all-loving God allow suffering in the world? [1]
2. **Any two from:** Job was targeted by Satan to experience great suffering; God sustained Job throughout; Job was blessed by God at the end of his suffering, including the blessing of a new family; suffering may be difficult but it can lead to a stronger faith [2]
3. **Any two from:** The God-given ability for humans to make their own decisions; this allows humans the ability to sin; Adam and Eve are the first example of this [2]
4. Suffering comes from either the denial of God or through selfish action [2]; this suffering can be overcome through human effort and through the intervention of divine grace (Gurprasad) [2]
5. **Any five from:** Adam and Eve were blessed with existence in the Garden of Eden; everything was available to them, except for the fruit of the tree of knowledge of good and evil; the temptation of the serpent led Eve and then Adam into sin; their sin caused them to hide from God; God punished the couple by expelling them from the garden; the curse of painful childbirth and having to work the land completed man's 'fall' from closeness with God; death entered the world as a consequence of sin [5]

Page 35

1. Baptism [1]; confirmation [1]
2. Catholics are able to confess their sins and ask for forgiveness [1]; this forgiveness may require actions of penance [1]
3. **Any two from:** They are sacraments that celebrate stages of life; both are church services; both services see promises made about belonging to Christianity [2]
4. Takes place when someone is either seriously ill or close to death [1]; the priest says a prayer of blessing to the Catholic believer [1]; this blessing helps to bring the believer close to Jesus, through His suffering [1]; it can help prepare someone for death (Extreme Unction) [1]
5. Marriage is a sacred contract made in front of God [1]; the commitment is a life-long promise of union [1]; divorce is not allowed between baptised Catholics [1]; it helps the Church to grow by providing a place for children to be born [1]; it reflects the union of Christ and the Church [1]

Page 36

1. A conversation between a believer and God [1]; a chance for a believer to connect with God, ask for help, pray for others, offer praise and worship, confess sins [1]
2. Rosary beads [1]; they can aid the memory, helping to recall prayers [1]
3. The Hail Mary or the Ave Maria [1]; it is based on Mary's meeting with the Angel Gabriel [1]
4. It can help focus prayer in four key areas: **A**doration, or how wonderful God is [1]; **C**onfession, or asking forgiveness for things for which the believer is sorry [1]; **T**hanksgiving, or time to reflect and say thank you for what God has done [1]; **S**upplication, or asking God to help [1]
5. Prayer can be individual and personal [1]; prayer can either be silent or spoken [1]; it can be pre-written or Spirit inspired [1]; some believers choose to kneel to pray while others may pray as they work [1]; many prayers can be a statement of faith, learned when a believer is young [1]

Page 37

1. **Any two from:** Bethlehem; Jerusalem; Lourdes; Nazareth; Walsingham; Rome; Taizé; Knock [2]
2. **Any two from:** To see the statue of the Virgin Mary; to drink or bathe in holy water; in the hope of being healed [2]
3. A believer can feel as though they have become closer to God [1]; there is time set aside for meditation and contemplation [1]
4. **Any four from:** It is not a holiday; it is a journey to a place of significance to a religion's history; a pilgrimage may be completed as penance for sin; a believer may journey in the hope of healing; pilgrimage can be carried out purely as an act of devotion [4]
5. **Any five from:** Most would visit the Holy Land; they would want to visit places recorded in the New Testament; visits could take place to: Bethlehem – Jesus' birthplace, Nazareth – the area where Jesus spent the majority of His life, Jerusalem – where Jesus worked during the majority of His ministry; Christians may also visit places such as Golgotha to remember Jesus' crucifixion; all of these places correlate with key events in Jesus' life, drawing the believer closer to Him [5]

Page 39 Quick Test
1. Omnipotent – all-powerful; omniscient – all-knowing; omnipresent – all present; omnibenevolent – all good / all loving; eternal – always been in existence
2. Polytheism
3. Monotheism – belief in one God; polytheism – belief in many gods
4. Own answer

Page 41 Quick Test
1. The birth, life, death and resurrection of Jesus and the subsequent spread of the Church.
2. Submission to the will of Allah

Page 43 Quick Test
1. Anyone can lead worship; however, it is often led by a minister, vicar or priest
2. Friday just after noon; an imam
3. Prayers are said, a sermon given, psalms are sung and scriptures are read

Page 45 Quick Test
1. Because Jesus promised to be with them when they did so
2. Sunday
3. Usually in church
4. Marks the death and resurrection of Jesus

Page 47 Quick Test
1. It contains 66 books written by a variety of authors
2. They believe that God speaks to them through its pages
3. Poetry, prophecy, history
4. It does not follow the same chronology as the others; appears to be more theological; treats the miracles and teaching of Jesus very differently

Page 49 Quick Test
1. Muhammad relayed the 'recitations' to his followers
2. After his death, Muhammad's teachings were collected together in what is now known as the Qur'an
3. The Tenakh contains the 39 books; the Talmud is the written version of the oral teaching
4. It is a collection of teachings and hymns written by a variety of Sikh Gurus over many years
5. Bathing before handling it; keeping it in its own room; carrying it above the head, etc.

Page 51 Quick Test
1. It is symbolic of Jesus' death
2. Obedience to the will of Allah; it gives them a spiritual experience; it is one of the Five Pillars of Islam
3. Obedience to strict scriptural teaching
4. Kesh (uncut hair); Kara (a steel bracelet); Kanga (a wooden comb); Kaccha (cotton underwear); Kirpan (steel sword)

Page 52
1. **Any one from:** God the Father; God the Son; God the Holy Spirit [1]
2. The power over all things, even outside of the laws of physics [1]
3. God the Father [1]
4. The universe was created perfectly [1]; humans were designed to work in harmony with each other [1]; God does not create evil, only good [1]; He has a plan for every life that is designed to bring the greatest amount of good [1]
5.

Agreeing with the statement	Against the statement
Most of the UK are atheist.	Most of the world believe in a god.
Too much suffering happens for God to exist.	The Holy Spirit is without physical form.
Many argue they have never seen or heard God.	Humans have free will to choose what they believe; some people believe that they have experienced God.
Other religions may believe in God but not the Holy Spirit.	Humans are responsible for their actions on Earth.

[Up to 3 marks for reasons in agreement; up to 3 marks in disagreement]

Page 53
1. 'The Word' [1]
2. **Any one from:** Matthew; Luke [1]
3. King Herod [1]
4. Jesus taught that loving God and loving each other are the best ways to live [1]; Christians believe Jesus was without sin – following this is the perfect example [1]; moral decisions can be made when following Jesus' example without prejudice [1]
5.

Agreeing with the statement	Against the statement
Christians should live their lives in the belief that they can make it to heaven in the afterlife.	Focusing on the afterlife can be seen as being selfish.
A heaven-focused life can lead to a moral life.	Christians can never be sure of what will happen after life.
Loving God and others should create a better world.	Jesus lived His life for others, not for Himself.
Jesus' resurrection and defeat of death is central to the Christian faith.	Christians are called to bring others to Christ and not just to focus on their own life.

[Up to 3 marks for reasons in agreement; up to 3 marks in disagreement]

Page 54
1. Reincarnation [1]
2. A funeral [1]
3. Purgatory [1]
4. Life should be lived to be good to others [1]; any act of good done to another will see good done unto you [1]; acts that wrong another will result in a negative impact on your life [1]; karma throughout an entire life is part of the judgement when reincarnation takes place [1]
5.

Agreeing with the statement	Against the statement
Population is higher than ever before and is still growing.	Cremation is forbidden in Islam.
Time and effort spent preparing graves could be better spent on providing for people still alive.	Families sometimes feel the need to have a specific place they can visit to remember a loved one.
Areas marked for burial could be used for other purposes – housing or farming.	Many people do not believe in the afterlife and want to prolong a connection with the deceased.
Only the soul lives on after death – so saving the body serves no purpose.	The space required to bury a body is very small.

[Up to 3 marks for reasons in agreement; up to 3 marks in disagreement]

Page 55
1. The Ten Commandments [1]
2. Heaven [1]
3. 'Do not murder.' [1]
4. Lucifer was an angel created by God [1]; he sought the praise of the other angels that should have been given to God [1]; God banished Lucifer from heaven [1]; other angels 'fell' with Lucifer and hell was created for them [1]
5.

Agreeing with the statement	Against the statement
We only have this life to make a difference.	The afterlife is a focus of every religion.
There may not be an afterlife.	Every life is the individual's to live.
Thinking about the next life could be selfish as it would lead to a self-centred focus.	If there is an afterlife and it has not been lived for, then the individual could end up in hell.
There is no certainty about which religion is right, if any.	Focusing on the afterlife can lead to someone being selfless by following their religion's teachings.

[Up to 3 marks for reasons in agreement; up to 3 marks in disagreement]

Page 56
1. Theodicy [1]
2. An act or thought contrary to the will of God [1]
3. Something that brings pain to humanity that was not designed by God [1]
4. The Garden of Eden was a perfect creation [1]; Adam and Eve could eat anything bar the fruit of the tree of knowledge of good and evil [1]; the serpent tempted Eve to eat the fruit, Eve then gave the fruit to Adam [1]; God saw their disobedience and threw them out of the garden [1]
5.

Agreeing with the statement	Against the statement
If God existed, He would stop the evil from happening.	Free will is a God-given ability to make our own choices as humans.
God can be used as an excuse for violence.	Evil acts are carried out at the hands of humans.
For God to exist, humanity would have been created by Him and would not act in the way it does.	God promised after the flood in Genesis that He would not act in the same way again.
An unloving God may have made a pain-filled Earth.	Some people harm themselves.

[Up to 3 marks for reasons in agreement; up to 3 marks in disagreement]

Page 57
1. Baptism [1]
2. Eucharist (Holy Communion) [1]   3.   An act of penance [1]
4. **Any four from:** It remembers the Last Supper that Jesus shared with the disciples; the bread remembers the body of Jesus; the wine is used to symbolise the blood that Jesus shed on the cross; Eucharist allows a Catholic to confess sins and draw closer to God; Catholicism: transubstantiation [4]
5. When a sin has been committed, a Catholic can confess it to their priest or bishop [1]; through this, they can find spiritual healing [1]; they have to show true remorse to be forgiven [1]; the priest can then give absolution, taking away the sin of the believer [1]; sanctification can follow as the believer makes amends for the sins committed [1]; anything shared during the confession is confidential and cannot be then shared by the priest [1]

Page 58
1. **Any one from:** The Lord's Prayer; Hail Mary [1]
2. **Any one from:** To show reverence to God; to grow closer to God; to learn God's will more fully [1]
3. Communal prayer [1]
4. **Any four from:** It allows communication with God; a Christian can confess their sins; they can thank God for blessings; ask for help for others; receive guidance for their future; express adoration for God [4]
5.

Agreeing with the statement	Against the statement
We all have the physical ability to act.	The Bible tells Christians to pray.
Many do not believe in the existence of God – so prayer would be pointless.	It allows God to show His power.
The prayer may not be answered so nothing happens.	It can stop the wrong decision being made by humans.
The prayer may not be in God's will.	Answered prayer can strengthen faith.

[Up to 3 marks for reasons in agreement; up to 3 marks in disagreement]

Page 59
1. A journey to a place of significance in a religion's history [1]
2. **Any one from:** Jerusalem; Bethlehem; Nazareth [1]
3. The Virgin Mary [1]
4. The grotto is believed to have healing powers [1]; Catholics can pray in front of the statue of the Virgin Mary [1]; many visitors expect to see a vision of the Virgin Mary [1]; others will take loved ones there in the hope that they may either draw near to God or be healed [1]

5.

Agreeing with the statement	Against the statement
Pilgrimage can be seen as being selfish.	Pilgrimage can strengthen someone to help others.
Visiting places from the past may not help the future.	Muslims are taught to complete Hajj.
Pilgrimage can be very expensive and the money could help lots of other people.	Being able to visit a place of pilgrimage can see someone being healed.
Religion teaches about putting others ahead of yourself.	Money from pilgrimage can help the local community.

[Up to 3 marks for reasons in agreement; up to 3 marks in disagreement]

Pages 60–67 **Practice Questions**

Page 60
1. A Christian declaration of faith [1]; it defines who Christians believe God is [1]
2. It is the power of God [1] manifested on Earth [1]
3. **Any two from:** Personal miracles and visions; the history of the Bible; the universe and its perceived design; morality; conscience [2]
4. Atheist – believes that there is no god [1]; agnostic – not sure whether there is a god or not [1]; monotheist – belief in one god [1]; polytheist – belief in more than one god [1]
5. Eternal – has not been created and will exist forever [1]; omniscient – all-knowing [1]; omnipresent – present everywhere at all times [1]; omnibenevolent – all good / all loving [1]; omnipotent – all powerful [1]

Page 61
1. A fact can be proven with evidence [1]; a belief cannot be proven, though there may be evidence to support it. [1]
2. There is no God but Allah [1]; Muhammad is the messenger of Allah [1]
3. **Any two from:** There is only one God; God is without form, or gender; everyone has direct access to God; everyone is equal before God [2]
4. Belief guides the decisions that they make [1]; shapes their everyday lives [1]; outlines their moral code [1]; provides a structure for how this life leads to eternal life [1]
5. **Any five from:** They believe that the name Yahweh is too holy to be spoken, so they remove the vowels; Jews believe that God knows all and can do anything; they follow the covenant made between Abraham and God; many Jews live their lives following the rules of the Torah, in the knowledge that judgement will come when they die; others believe judgement takes place on Earth; Jews are still waiting for the Messiah to descend to Earth. [5]

Page 62
1. **Any two from:** Adoration; acts of religious praise, honour or devotion; giving glory to God [2]
2. Christians share bread and wine as part of Communion [1]; Sikhs share the sacred food of Kara Parshad [1]
3. The rabbi will lead the worship with readings from the Torah [1]; no instruments are played but the cantor leads the singing [1]
4. **Any four from:** Prayer (individual and collective); songs; readings from scripture; declarations of faith; teaching from scripture (sermons); can convey key teachings; may include the sacrament of Holy Communion [4]
5. **Any five from:** Shoes and socks are removed upon arrival; Muslim men complete the washing ritual of wudu; this involves the washing of the arms, hands, face, feet and head; prayers take place underneath the zulla (the prayer hall); all members face towards Mecca to pray; the imam will deliver teaching from the Qur'an [5]

Page 63
1. It can aid the ability to praise and thank God [1]; and enter into God's presence [1]
2. Christians share bread and wine as part of Holy Communion [1]; they remember Jesus' death and resurrection [1]
3. Celebrates the Holy Spirit coming to Earth [1]; reminds Christians that God's power can help them [1]

4. They are directed to in the Bible [1]; it provides time in fellowship together [1]; it is a time to thank God [1]; it is a time to praise God [1]

5. They allow Christians to connect with key events from the past [1]; a festival can bring congregations together [1]; festivals can provide opportunities for forgiveness [1]; some people can find new belief in God through festivals [1]; Easter and Christmas are at the centre of Christianity [1]

Page 64

1. **Any two from:** It is the Word of God; some Christians see the Bible as being a perfect record of God; it contains the teachings of God and Jesus [2]

2. The Old Testament [1] and the New Testament [1]

3. Old Testament – Hebrew [1]; New Testament – Greek [1]

4. The historical books [1]; the Pentateuch [1]; the poetic books [1]; the prophetical books [1]

5. **Any five from:** Christians believe that they can find guidance in the Bible; God can speak directly to a Christian through the words of the Bible; reading the Bible collectively can bring Christians together in worship; the Bible can be used as part of a daily devotional routine; Christians can learn about the history of their religion; teachings about morality can be applied to everyday life; Christians can learn more about God's character [5]

Page 65

1. Guru Nanak [1]; another nine authors [1]

2. A period of 48 hours of continuous reading of the Guru Granth Sahib [1]; the reading is led by a team of readers from the Gurdwara [1]

3. Arabic [1] and Hebrew [1]

4. The Torah [1], the Nevi'im [1] and the Ketuvim [1]; 39 books in total [1]

5. **Any five from:** They can learn about the history of their religion; a believer can learn from the mistakes of those who have gone before them; a holy book can provide guidance on important decisions in life; prayers can be learned and recited; they can come together in fellowship to read their holy book; a believer may be taught to read the scripture in its original language [5]

Page 66–67

1. Sabbath (Shabbat) [1]; between sunset Friday and sunset Saturday [1]

2. **Any two from:** Rosh Hashanah (New Year); Yom Kippur (Day of Atonement); Pesach (Passover); Shavuot (Feast of Weeks); Sukkott (Feast of Booths); Hanukkah [2]

3. **Any two from:** Brit Milah; Bar and Bat Mitzvah; Marriage; Death [2]

4. A day of rest without work [1]; a time to worship [1]

5. Many children died young [1]; baptism allowed the children to be offered to God [1] before they were old enough to make decisions for themselves [1]

6. Baptism/christening [1]; confirmation [1]; marriage [1]; funeral [1]

7. Shahadah – the statement of belief at the heart of the Muslim faith (daily) [1]; Zakah – giving 2.5% of income away (weekly, monthly or annually) [1]; Hajj – pilgrimage to Mecca, at least once in a lifetime [1]; Salah – praying five times a day (daily) [1]; Sawm – fasting through the month of Ramadan [1]

Pages 68–79 **Revise Questions**

Page 69 Quick Test

1. Story with a hidden meaning told by Jesus

2. Poverty; humility; child-like faith; servant-nature

3. Sacrifice

4. Suggested by William Wrede to explain why Jesus wasn't more readily recognised during his ministry

Page 71 Quick Test

1. The heavens parted; the Holy Spirit descended; a heavenly voice announces Him as the Son of God.

2. Peter describes Him as Messiah (the Christ)

3. Judas Iscariot

Page 73 Quick Test

1. Healing; nature; resurrections

2. Response to faith; power over nature; compassion; sign of the Good News

3. Casting out unclean spirits

4. Power over nature

5. Compassion for others

Page 75 Quick Test

1. Authority; blasphemy; Sabbath; taxes

2. Triumphal entry; palm leaves waved; Jesus rode on a donkey; cleansed Temple; conflict with leaders

3. Jesus shared bread and wine with the disciples, announcing that the bread was His body and the wine was His blood; He warned them of the coming betrayal by one of the 12.

Page 77 Quick Test

1. He is 'Most Gracious' and 'Most Merciful' and is to be worshipped

2. The good news of future rewards

3. Lesser Jihad is armed battle/collective defence; Greater Jihad is a peaceful battle for self-control

Page 79 Quick Test

1. He is credited with setting up the Ka'ba in Mecca as a place of pilgrimage

2. The sins of adultery and murder attributed to him

Pages 80–87 **Review Questions**

Page 80

1. A religion that believes in a single God [1]   2. An agnostic [1]

3. To be God, He cannot have been created and will always exist [1]

4. **Any four from:** It sets out how churches and Christians should act; it sets out the end times; it prophesies that God will bring judgement on the world; the book shows that He will protect those who follow Him; the world will end and God will remove all evil [4]

5.

Agreeing with the statement	Against the statement
Religion is about faith and not fact.	Personal faith can prove God's experience.
Humans have spent thousands of years trying to write arguments to do so and have failed.	The existence or non-existence of God will be known upon death.
Advances in science suggest that there is more likelihood that His existence will be disproved.	If God wanted to be known, He would allow it to happen.
We don't have the means to test for God as He is not physical.	Many Christians believe that the Bible has proved God's existence.

[Up to 3 marks for reasons in agreement; up to 3 marks in disagreement]

Page 81

1. Muhammad [1]

2. The vowels, so that it could not be spoken [1]

3. Kosher [1]

4. Allah is the only God [1]; He chose to reveal Himself through the Prophet Muhammad [1]; He is the creator of all [1]; submission to the will of Allah is the main goal for a Muslim. [1]

5.

Agreeing with the statement	Against the statement
Science has proven many religious beliefs to be incorrect.	Religion can be just as significant today as it was when the scriptures were written.
The varied range of religious beliefs can cause conflict.	Beliefs can help to shape and guide decisions.
Scripture can give little guidance on medical issues such as euthanasia and abortion.	Many religious believers would argue that religious morals can lead to a better world.
A religious believer may choose to follow their own personal beliefs after prayer.	Most of the world's knowledge is ancient, in particular mathematical understanding.

[Up to 3 marks for reasons in agreement; up to 3 marks in disagreement]

Page 82

1. Friday [1]   2. The Sabbath [1]

3. Kara Parshad [1]

4. **Any four from:** Prayer – either private or collective; song – used to declare beliefs, feelings, praise or thanksgiving; readings – passages from scripture can be read; sermons – sections of scriptures can be used to provide teaching; meditation – periods of quietness allow for reflection; service [4]

5.

Agreeing with the statement	Against the statement
Religious believers are called to love others and help those in need.	Sikhs help others by offering food in the langar hall.
Time spent in a holy building separates religious believers from the rest of their community.	Spending time in worship helps to build the faith of the religious believer.
Worship can lead to a religious believer forgetting about the situations around the world that they could be helping with.	Praying for others during worship can allow God to change their lives for the better.
Focusing on the needs of one religion can cause arguments with other faiths.	Collections, or donating money during worship, can help others. Some believers work with religious charities.

[Up to 3 marks for reasons in agreement; up to 3 marks in disagreement]

Page 83
1. Sunday [1]
2. Pentecost [1]
3. The pulpit [1]
4. **Any four from:** Many of the Church's early Christians were born as Jews; they were brought up worshipping in the synagogue; primitive worship centred solely on the Bible; songs later came out, initially through the Psalms; early Christians met in houses and other buildings, special buildings for worship came later. [4]

5.

Agreeing with the statement	Against the statement
Prayer allows conversation with God.	All forms of worship are important, not only prayer.
Prayer gives time to thank and praise.	Holy Communion could be argued as the most important part of worship, as it remembers Jesus' death and resurrection.
Jesus practised prayer many times.	It could also be argued that reading the Bible is most vital in worship.

[Up to 3 marks for reasons in agreement; up to 3 marks in disagreement]

Page 84
1. As the inspired Word of God [1]
2. The lives and works of the first disciples and the beginnings of the early Church [1]
3. They can follow the laws laid out within it [1]; they can try to put into practice the teachings of Jesus [1]; mistakes from the past can be learned from [1]; principles such as love and putting others first can guide the right course of action [1]

4.

Agreeing with the statement	Against the statement
Some events are omitted from some of the Gospels.	The Gospels were written for different audiences.
The Gospels focus on some elements in much greater detail than others.	Matthew and John were disciples, so had different insights into the life of Jesus.
John's Gospel starts differently to the Synoptic Gospels.	Different eyewitness accounts would have been used when the Gospels were written.
When comparing sources, discrepancies can raise questions over authenticity.	The Gospels were not written at the same time, which allows for a change in focus.

[Up to 3 marks for reasons in agreement; up to 3 marks in disagreement]

Page 85
1. The angel Gabriel appeared and revealed the will of Allah to him [1]
2. **Any one from:** The Torah; Books of Moses; Pentateuch [1]
3. Guru Gobind Singh [1]

4. **Any four from:** The scrolls are always handwritten; if a single mistake is made, the section of parchment has to be re-started; the scrolls are kept in the Ark in the synagogue; they are read from the bimah by a male over 13; it is not touched by hand; a yad is used when reading [4]
5. Sikhs recognise the Guru Granth Sahib as a living book [1]; it was left as the guide after the death of Guru Gobind Singh, the tenth Guru [1]; Sikhs will bathe before they handle the book [1]; to show its importance, the book has its own room for when it is not being read [1]; it is carried above head height and feet are kept below it [1]; a Sikh will always consult the book before making an important decision [1]

Page 86–87
1. Kashrut/Kosher [1]
2. Bar Mitzvah [1]
3. The Shahadah [1]
4. Halal [1]; the blood of the animal has to be drained during preparation [1]
5. **Any four from:** It supports people who are less well-off; as part of the Five Pillars it is decreed by the Qur'an; it helps Islam to support itself; the money shared can help to spread the Islamic religion; it helps to develop sacrifice and selflessness [4]
6. **Any six from:** They will seek to help others; money will be given to charity; time will be spent studying scripture; prayer meetings during the week may be attended and Sundays will see them worship at church; evangelical Christians actively try to persuade others to become Christians; some Christians study for years to become priests, vicars or ministers; nuns and monks are Christians who have withdrawn from everyday life to concentrate on prayer or serving the poor. [6]

Pages 88–93 Practice Questions

Page 88
1. **Any suitable answers, e.g.** The Son of God; Saviour; the 'anointed one' [2]
2. He used parables [1] taking situations that the crowds would understand to explain religious teachings. [1]
3. **Any two from:** A future king coming in glory; demonstrates humanity, one who came down amongst us and showed God as truly human; humility [2]
4. The Kingdom of God [1]; discipleship [1]; titles of Jesus [1]; the 'Messianic Secret' [1]
5. He would have been arrested much earlier [1]; He had to fulfil the prophecies from the Old Testament [1]; Jesus wanted as many as possible to hear His teachings [1]; inciting crowds would have turned them away [1]; declaring who He was during His trial was part of the prophecy fulfilment [1]

Page 89
1. To be drawn to an individual [1] and follow their teachings and way of life [1]
2. **Any two from:** It is the shortest Gospel and ends quickly with a sense of urgency; there are no birth stories and the resurrection accounts are shorter than in the other Gospels; it is the nearest thing we have to an eyewitness account [2]
3. As the Messiah [1] and the Son of God [1]
4. He called them from a range of backgrounds [1]; the disciples were part of different socio-economic groups [1]; men were chosen as the society of the day would not have listened to women [1]; Jesus knew how their skills would work together [1]
5. **Any five from:** The disciples travel with Jesus to Caesarea Philippi; Peter, James and John are with Jesus; Moses and Elijah are seen with Jesus; Jesus is seen as being God for the first time; God declares, 'this is my Son'; Moses and Elijah represent the Law and the Prophets and show the continuity brought by Jesus [5]

Page 90
1. An event attributed to divine intervention [1]; a supernatural event outside of the laws of nature [1]
2. **Any two from:** Nature miracles; healing miracles and exorcisms; resurrections [2]
3. When someone who has died [1] is raised back to life [1]
4. **Any four from:** Stilling the storm (4:35-41); feeding the five thousand (6:30-46); walking on water (6:47-56); feeding the four thousand (8:1-9); withering the fig tree (11:20-25) [4]
5. They show God's power [1]; miracles can show that Jesus was the Son of God [1]; healing miracles show that Jesus had compassion for those in suffering [1]; nature miracles point to God having

created the universe [1]; Christians believe that miracles can happen today [1]

Page 91

1. Where an individual claims that they are a form of deity and equal to God – the crime Jesus was crucified for [1]; speaking disrespectfully against God [1]
2. Mark 1:22 [1] and 11:28 [1]
3. **Any two from:** It began Holy Week; Jesus entered Jerusalem on a donkey; His arrival was celebrated with the scattering of palm branches [2]
4. Christians share in Holy Communion/Eucharist [1]; the service reflects elements of the Last Supper, quoting Jesus' words [1]; bread and wine are shared [1]; prayers of penance and requests of forgiveness are made, based upon Jesus' sacrifice and resurrection [1]
5. **Any five from:** After being abused by soldiers, Jesus was taken to be crucified; Simon of Cyrene was forced to carry His cross to Golgotha, the place of execution; He was crucified between two criminals; there was darkness between noon and three o'clock; Jesus cried out: 'Eloi, Eloi, lama sabachthani?' (meaning: 'My God, my God, why have you forsaken me?'); with a loud cry, He died; the Temple curtain was torn in two from top to bottom; some of the women watched as His body was placed in a tomb donated by Joseph of Arimathea [5]

Page 92

1. There is no God but Allah [1]; He has the most beautiful names [1]
2. Lesser Jihad – the Islamic fight against evil in the world [1]; Greater Jihad – the personal fight in a Muslim's life against evil [1]
3. **Any two from:** 'The path to the watering hole'; Islamic law; the laws for living laid out in the Qur'an and the Hadith [2]
4. The story is similar to that in Judaism and Christianity [1]; Allah created the universe in six days [1]; Adam sprang to life after being moulded from the earth and clay [1]; Adam and Eve lived in paradise before they sinned [1]
5. **Any five from:** Allah cherishes and sustains the world and should be worshipped; Allah is Most Merciful and Most Gracious – Muslims can ask Allah for help to find the 'straight way'; the Tawhid outlines the 'oneness of Allah' – Allah is the only God and is singular; Allah is omniscient, omnipotent and transcendent; if one aims to associate with Allah and gain equality, this is known as shirk (idolatry); Muslims can draw closer to Allah by reciting the 99 beautiful names taught by Muhammad. [5]

Page 93

1. A faithful messenger [1]; a believer in the oneness of God [1]
2. Warning his father to stop worshipping idols [1]; forming the Ka'ba in Mecca as a place of pilgrimage [1]
3. Sulaiman is seen as the son of Dawud, a king of Israel [1]; he was a divinely appointed king and a gifted prophet [1]
4. Maryam (Mary) [1]; seen to be a virgin [1]; the Qur'an records details of her birth, childhood and the birth of Isa [1]; she is regarded as being a role model for Muslims to follow [1]
5. **Any five from:** Isa is a prophet of Allah – however he is not divine; Allah gave Isa the task of leading the Jewish people in a new scripture; his birth was designed by Allah to be a virginal conception; Isa is separated from the other prophets of Islam as he was blessed with the ability to perform miracles; he was also the only prophet not to marry or father children; Isa was a Muslim who did not die but ascended to join Allah in heaven [5]

Pages 94–109 Revise Questions

Page 95 Quick Test

1. Jesus shows His power over nature; Jesus overcomes human illness
2. Account of John's visions
3. Seeing memories of the past and a tunnel with a bright light at the end

Page 97 Quick Test

1. The sixth day
2. In the image of God
3. The eternal aspect of ourselves; the essence of who we are

Page 99 Quick Test

1. Genesis 1:27; 1 Corinthians 3:16; Psalm 139:13
2. Some Jews argue that life is fully granted after 40 days of pregnancy
3. Some Muslims believe that this occurs at 40 days, some at 120 days and others when there is voluntary movement of the foetus

Page 101 Quick Test

1. Some believers would argue that life is not being protected and not valued in the way that a gift from God should be.
2. Artificial insemination by husband (AIH); artificial insemination by donor (AID)
3. Issues about sanctity of life; playing God

Page 103 Quick Test

1. Marriage contract; promises before God; witnesses
2. The Catholic Church does not allow divorce or remarriage; however, an annulment is sometimes granted.

Page 105 Quick Test

1. Faith education; a good example; stability; a model laid out by God in Genesis 1
2. Different types of family groupings are more common
3. Fewer cases of divorce; less cohabitation; faith education; more marriage; worship attendance

Page 107 Quick Test

1. In dedication, no promises are made on behalf of the child; water is also absent from the ceremony
2. Guidance; development; faith; caring example; protection
3. Maturity; own promises

Page 109 Quick Test

1. Christianity; Sikhism
2. 'Mercy-killing'; a gentle death
3. Execution; capital punishment

Pages 110–115 Review Questions

Page 110

1. **Any one from:** The question asking why others did not recognise Jesus as the Son of God; the thought that Jesus kept His identity secret [1]
2. Jesus called His first disciple [1]
3. Humility [1]
4. **Any four from:** No lamp would be hidden under a bowl; it would be put on a stand for all to see; therefore, all should listen carefully to Jesus' teachings; the more that they listen, the more they will be able to understand; share your faith to help others [4]
5.

Agreeing with the statement	Against the statement
If Jesus was not God, then His parables had no authority.	Jesus' parables include many key moral teachings.
The stories focus on ideals.	Christianity still seeks to follow the teachings.
Many of the principles can be found in other religions.	Jesus lived out the teachings from His own parables.
The context may no longer be relevant.	The teachings, like the Ten Commandments, do not age.

[Up to 3 marks for reasons in agreement; up to 3 marks in disagreement]

Page 111

1. Thomas [1]
2. The news of the coming of the Kingdom of God and of Jesus' death and resurrection to restore people's relationship with God [1]
3. A fisherman [1]
4. **Any four from:** He knew that only teaching crowds would not be enough; the disciples would carry on His work after His ascension; the disciples were called from different areas of society; the Gospels needed the disciples and their peers in order to record the events of Jesus' ministry; an example of how God wants personal relationships [4]

5.

Agreeing with the statement	Against the statement
Jesus could have called anyone but only called men.	Women were second-class citizens at the time of Jesus. It would have been socially unacceptable.
There have only ever been male popes.	Jesus spent much of his time with women.
Having chosen 12, two could easily have been women.	Much of the New Testament outside of the Gospels raised the profile and value of women.
The vast majority of prophets were male too.	Recent changes in the appointment of female priests and bishops shows the practice behind Jesus' teachings.

[Up to 3 marks for reasons in agreement; up to 3 marks in disagreement]

Page 112
1. Jesus heals Simon's mother-in-law [1]
2. **Any one from:** They suggested that He was the Son of God; they thought He was being blasphemous [1]
3. The crowd begged Jesus to touch the deaf man [1]; Jesus put His fingers into the man's ears and spat onto his tongue [1]; the man was able to hear and speak freely [1]; Jesus told the crowd not to tell anyone about what they had seen. [1]

4.

Agreeing with the statement	Against the statement
Actions like this will have added to pressure to have Jesus crucified.	Jesus saw the need to heal and decided that it was greater than the law of the Sabbath.
Jesus could have performed the miracles on any other day.	He purposefully challenged the laws of the Sabbath.
He could have performed the miracles out of view.	The miracles showed His power and needed to be seen.
Jesus knew the impact that His actions would have had.	Healing is not working.

[Up to 3 marks for reasons in agreement; up to 3 marks in disagreement]

Page 113
1. Execution of an individual by attaching them to a wooden cross [1]
2. Judas Iscariot [1]
3. The Sanhedrin [1]
4. Palm Sunday [1]; Maundy Thursday [1]; Good Friday [1]; Holy Saturday [1]

5.

Agreeing with the statement	Against the statement
Creates the hope that there is more than this life.	If God created the universe, He created the laws of physics and biology.
Resurrection is physically impossible.	Without the resurrection, a lot of hope is lost.
It could be argued that the Bible in its entirety is a helpful guide for life.	Many Christians believe that it shows God's love for humanity.
The proof of the resurrection does not exist.	The Passion Week fulfils the prophecies of the Old Testament.

[Up to 3 marks for reasons in agreement; up to 3 marks in disagreement]

Page 114
1. 99 [1]   2. Tawhid [1]   3. Shirk [1]
4. The Lesser Jihad is the fight against worldwide issues [1]; a Muslim must defend and promote their faith [1]; the Greater Jihad is a

personal, inner battle [1]; they must follow the teachings of the Qur'an and resist the pressures of the world [1]

5.

Agreeing with the statement	Against the statement
With Islam being a younger religion, replication could be argued for.	The creation story may be accurate, with various religions trying to claim it as their own.
Many of the details seem too similar to not be a replication.	Muslims could argue that the Qur'anic account is more accurate as Muhammad is the only dictator of the words of the Qur'an as opposed to the numerous authors of the Tenakh and the Bible.
Science has presented the Big Bang theory in opposition to the creation story.	There is no way of proving whether any of the creation stories are accurate or not.
Examples such as dinosaurs highlight weaknesses in the creation story.	Similarities between the accounts do not prove any are inaccurate.

[Up to 3 marks for reasons in agreement; up to 3 marks in disagreement]

Page 115
1. To build an ark [1]   2. They drowned [1]   3. Hagar [1]
4. Prophets can give specific instructions [1]; these instructions can be given to specific people at specific times [1]; prophets can also speak to individuals face to face [1]; the words of prophets can also reinforce the teachings of the Qur'an [1]

5.

Agreeing with the statement	Against the statement
The Qur'an and the Khalif contain all of the key teachings.	Some could argue that the teachings of new prophets could be more easily disproved.
Anyone now claiming to be a prophet with new teachings could be considered a heretic.	There may be modern day prophets sent by Allah but with a message only for a few people.
With media technologies, any new prophet could spread their message very quickly.	New teachings or guidance may be revealed on a personal level.
Islam is growing rapidly without any new instruction.	It may be possible that some imams are prophets.

[Up to 3 marks for reasons in agreement; up to 3 marks in disagreement]

Pages 116–123 Practice Questions

Page 116
1. **Any two from:** Miracles; visions; near-death experiences; conversion [2]
2. **Any two from:** Exorcisms; nature and healing miracles; resurrections [2]
3. Abraham [1]; he will have many descendants despite his age/God will protect him/his reward will be great [1]
4. It is different to all of the other 65 books [1]; John records his visions about the end times [1]; it reveals the end of this Earth and its judgement [1]; John sees the second coming of Christ and life after this world [1]
5. A large crowd listened to Him speak [1]; the disciples said the crowd were hungry [1]; Jesus commanded the disciples to ask the crowd for food [1]; a boy offered five loaves and two fishes [1]; Jesus blessed the food and there was more than enough to feed the 5000 people [1]

Page 117
1. On the sixth day [1]; God said it was 'very good' as opposed to just 'good' [1]
2. **Any two from:** They are made in God's image; because of this, they have a soul; they are given dominion over the rest of creation [2]
3. **Any two from:** A spiritual element of a human that is God-given; the essence of a person; it lives on after this life into eternity [2]

4. A decision has to be made as to when the life of a human begins [1]; if at birth then abortion is permissible [1]; if at conception then ending the pregnancy could be seen as murder [1]; for a Muslim, abortion may be permissible before 120 days of the pregnancy (when the soul is given to the life) [1]

5. **Any five from:** Jeremiah 1:5 states that God knew each life before it was born; each life is given a plan/design before birth; Job 12:10 states all life is held within God's hands; John 3:16 declares that God sacrificed Jesus to save mankind from sin; this latter verse shows how God values the human above all else; Ten Commandments – do not kill; man was made in God's image [5]

Page 118

1. It shows that God created humanity [1] and made them in His image [1]
2. At 40 days/120 days/when there is voluntary movement of the foetus [1]; when Allah gives the life its soul [1]
3. Many believe that life starts at conception [1]; they argue that when the egg is fertilised, life has been given by God [1]; at this point God gives the life its soul [1]; reference to Psalm 139:13 [1]
4. Choose not to have abortions themselves [1]; campaign against embryology practices [1]; support charities such as the Society for the Protection of Unborn Children [1]; refuse to use the morning after pill [1]; encourage those seeking abortions to consider adoptions instead [1]

Page 119

1. It shows that God is part of creation [1]; God knows each individual and sets them apart from the rest of creation [1]
2. Artificial insemination by husband [1]; the husband's sperm is used during the in-vitro fertilisation (IVF) process [1]
3. Most religious believers hold that life is given by God [1]; many believe that AIH is a good use of science [1]; some would argue that AID borders on adultery [1]; some Christians would argue that all people should have equal access to IVF [1]
4. The pregnant woman has to provide reasons as to why she wants to terminate the pregnancy [1]; two doctors have to agree to her request [1]; an abortion has to take place before 24 weeks of the pregnancy have passed [1]; pregnancies can still be ended in extreme cases after 24 weeks (such as where continuing the pregnancy is a serious risk to the mother's health or it is found that the child would be born with a severe handicap) [1]; the mother can meet the doctors alone [1]

Page 120

1. **Any two from:** When a marriage is ended; and it is as though it has never happened; not a divorce [2]
2. They are a public showing of unity [1]; they are a symbol of an eternal bond [1]
3. The wife is accepted into a family that will care for her [1]; the parents can help their offspring choose good life partners [1]
4. **Any four from:** Takes place in a synagogue; the rabbi will conduct the ceremony; prayers will be said by the couple and the congregation; scriptures are read as rings are exchanged; the ceremony takes place under a canopy called a chuppah; ketubah signed [4]

Page 121

1. **Any two from:** Financial pressures of the Western world; having to work on Sundays and finding time to attend their holy building; being a single parent brings greater pressure again [2]
2. They are not to antagonise their children [1]; they are to bring them up within the faith [1]
3. Husband and wife living together [1]; children living at home with their parents [1]
4. Platonic (friendships) [1]; family [1]; workplace [1]; sexual [1]
5. **Any five from:** Husbands are often the head of the family; they are seen to be responsible for providing for the family financially; wives are charged with looking after the home and raising the children; husbands should love their wives as Christ loves the Church; however, men and women are equal; parents should care and provide for their children, and children should respect and obey their parents [5]

Page 122

1. Children are a gift (reward) from God [1]; it implies they should be cared for [1]
2. They should come close to Him [1]; Kingdom of Heaven belongs to them [1]
3. Once they have been baptised [1]; typically around the age of 7 or soon after [1]

4. After birth, ceremonies take place to thank God for the child [1]; some children are dedicated – the parents, godparents and congregation thank God for the child, and promise to bring them up in the Church [1]; others are baptised – in addition to dedication, promises are made on the child's behalf to grow up in the Christian faith [1]; confirmation allows the child to make these promises in front of the congregation for themselves [1]

5. **Any five from:** The family should pray together and parents should pray for their children; time should be spent reading the Bible together; the family should attend church together; festivals such as Christmas, Easter and Pentecost should be celebrated in the home; parents and children should discuss important issues together; parents should share religious teachings on moral and ethical issues [5]

Page 123

1. Often a friend or family member helps [1] someone who is ill to end their life [1]
2. Active euthanasia requires medication or action to be given [1], whereas passive requires the removal of treatment [1]
3. China [1], with about 2000–4000 per year being carried out [1]
4. **Any four from:** The body is never left alone; the body is prepared in a simple linen shroud; organs cannot be removed from the body; the ceremony takes place in the synagogue as soon as possible; the body is buried after the funeral [4]
5. The body may be visited by the family [1]; an open coffin may be used during the funeral service [1]; the funeral service is often held in a church [1]; prayers of blessing are said as part of a celebration of life [1]; the body can be either buried or cremated [1]

Page 125 Quick Test

1. All things must have been 'caused'; the universe around us could not have just 'happened'
2. No-one would question a watch has been designed and made; many would argue that the same applies to a rock, as a rock could not exist as a result of an accident
3. Personal evaluation

Page 127 Quick Test

1. Conventional warfare – fought on the ground using soldiers; unconventional warfare – fought from a distance using missiles (WMD), etc.
2. Greed; money; land; power; ideology
3. Have a just cause; be declared by a lawful authority; have a good intention; be a last resort; have a reasonable chance of success; use proportional force to win; bring about more good than the harm that it causes

Page 129 Quick Test

1. Pacifism – opposed to conflict and its support; conscientious objection – opposed to violence but will offer peaceful support/will object to a specific conflict.
2. StWC has fought to bring an end to war throughout the world and find ways to influence governments and policies
3. The Geneva Convention set out the rights of civilians, prisoners of war and injured soldiers during a time of war; 159 articles designed to protect those not active during any conflict

Page 131 Quick Test

1. Protection; deterrence; reformation; retribution; reparation; vindication
2. A victim of crime may lose their life or possessions or may suffer physical or psychological harm; people feel unsafe
3. Execution

Page 133 Quick Test

1. Being very poor
2. **Any suitable answer, e.g.:** Christian Aid; Tearfund; CAFOD; Muslim Aid; World Jewish Relief
3. Natural disasters are events in nature, which can cause devastation and loss of life, e.g. earthquakes, floods, volcanoes and tornados.

Page 135 Quick Test

1. Some churches have appointed female priests and bishops, giving men and women equal opportunities to hold positions of authority in the Church.
2. Race; skin colour; religion; gender; poverty; disability; sexual orientation
3. My neighbour is anyone in need; to show selfless love to others, even my enemy

Page 137 Quick Test
1. To ensure that individuals were protected from harm under law; to protect basic human rights and aim to stop persecution, while allowing freedom of movement and of speech
2. It campaigns to end abuses of human rights and seeks justice for those whose rights have been violated.
3. 1977
4. It makes it unlawful for UK public bodies to act in ways which are incompatible with the European Convention on Human Rights.

Pages 138–145 Review Questions

Page 138
1. They help to reveal God's will [1]
2. Jesus calmed a storm on Lake Galilee [1]
3. They reveal something about God [1]; they can suggest what the afterlife is like [1]; common similarities suggest they are authentic [1]; they can show how God restores people even after death [1]
4.

Agreeing with the statement	Against the statement
Scientific knowledge is much stronger now and could provide explanations.	Miracles do not need to be broadcast globally for them to have happened.
All religious scriptures cannot be proven to be accurate.	Many miracles could only be performed by Jesus.
There are laws in science that cannot be broken.	Many events can still not be explained by science.
Miracles are often open to interpretation.	Some healings might still be miracles even with medical staff involvement.

[Up to 3 marks for reasons in agreement; up to 3 marks in disagreement]

Page 139
1. The premature termination of a pregnancy [1]
2. **Any two from:** The belief that God has given life; so only He has the right to take it away; life is precious, sacred, set apart [2]
3. It is a declaration of who Jesus was [1]; the verse reveals the sacrifice of Jesus [1]; Christians can see the path to forgiveness and heaven because of the verse [1]; it sets Christianity apart from other religions [1]
4.

Agreeing with the statement	Against the statement
Hospices aim to bring comfort for those near the end of their lives and provide support to the bereaved too.	Active euthanasia allows suffering, which hospices cannot always eradicate, to be brought to an end.
They provide opportunities for individuals to spend time with their families.	It protects family members from criminal prosecution if they want to help a loved one to die by taking them to another country.
Most hospices are charities, so do not cost the taxpayer.	Active euthanasia prevents any financial pressure on families or the taxpayer.
It helps to protect the rights of the elderly.	The UK should seek to be equal with other countries such as Switzerland and Holland.

[Up to 3 marks for reasons in agreement; up to 3 marks in disagreement]

Page 140
1. The Muslim name for the soul [1]
2. 40 days [1]
3. A sperm fertilises an egg [1]

4.

Agreeing with the statement	Against the statement
UK law recognises that life begins at birth.	Some may argue that religious views, e.g. life beginning at conception, should be taken into account under abortion law.
A mother can opt for an abortion or termination almost up to term.	A Christian can object to their embryos being used.
Embryos can be tested on up to 14 days of age.	A Muslim may only have an abortion before 40 or 120 days' gestation.
Anything removed during an abortion is seen as medical waste.	Catholics may campaign against all abortions.

[Up to 3 marks for reasons in agreement; up to 3 marks in disagreement]

Page 141
1. In-vitro fertilisation [1]
2. Up to 24 weeks [1]
3. A number of eggs are provided by either the female or a female donor [1]; sperm is provided by either the male or a male donor [1]; each egg is fertilised in a laboratory [1]; the eggs are placed inside the womb of the female [1]
4.

Agreeing with the statement	Against the statement
The pill ends a pregnancy if one has begun.	An egg may not have been fertilised.
The intention of taking the pill is to ensure that a baby is not born.	It does not need the agreement of two doctors for it to be given.
Christians believe that life starts at conception, not when the embryo implants on the womb.	Muslims believe that life begins at 120 days, so the morning after pill is not abortion.
The pill has to be obtained from a pharmacy and cannot be issued in the same way as the contraceptive pill.	The morning after pill does not need to be given by a doctor.

[Up to 3 marks for reasons in agreement; up to 3 marks in disagreement]

Page 142
1. To show respect [1] and show their acceptance of marital duties [1]
2. To show love and commitment [1]; to be able to have sex [1]; to have children [1]; to make a public declaration in front of God. [1]
3.

Agreeing with the statement	Against the statement
Marriage should only be ended by death.	Abuse may have become part of a marriage.
Catholic tradition forbids remarriage in the church.	Some churches believe that an individual may find love for the second time.
If divorced, an individual does not necessarily need to remarry.	Someone may have married their first partner before they became a Christian.
If children have been born in the marriage, remarriage may make things more difficult.	The Bible does not forbid remarriage.

[Up to 3 marks for reasons in agreement; up to 3 marks in disagreement]

Page 143
1. 'Honour your father and mother.' (Exodus 20:12) [1]
2. **Any one from:** Equality in the family; shared responsibility [1]
3. A couple, the children they have had together and their children from previous relationships [1]
4. Husband's job used to be the main source of income [1]; wives would usually stay at home to look after the house and the children [1]; these roles can now be shared [1]; wives can also either have the main career or their own career [1]

5.

Agreeing with the statement	Against the statement
Christians should only have sex within marriage.	Many single parents make brilliant mums/dads.
Two parents can help to provide a stable family home.	There can be abuse in marriage.
Children can benefit from the experience and love of two people.	Being married does not make someone a good parent.
Many biblical characters are shown in the traditional family setting of marriage.	Many UK marriages end in divorce, which can often be difficult for the child.

[Up to 3 marks for reasons in agreement; up to 3 marks in disagreement]

Page 144

1. Dedication **[1]**   2. Easter **[1]**
3. **Any one from:** Pray with them; read the Bible with them **[1]**
4. Infant baptism does not appear in the Bible **[1]**; dedication sees promises made by the parents, godparents and the congregation **[1]**; no promises are made on behalf of the child **[1]**; dedication focuses on thanks for the child as opposed to the future **[1]**
5.

Agreeing with the statement	Against the statement
Children spend time learning about Christianity.	Many Christians do not belong to a denomination that follows the teachings of confirmation.
It allows them to speak to other children at the meetings and share their experiences.	Confirmation may not be required for a Christian to start taking Holy Communion at their church.
It helps them to see the importance of the vows that were made by their parents during baptism.	Many churches follow the Alpha course to help deepen and further understanding of Christianity.
The process of confirmation can also be helpful for adults who have become Christians.	Some Christians may not feel the need to be confirmed if they were baptised as a child.

[Up to 3 marks for reasons in agreement; up to 3 marks in disagreement]

Page 145

1. The termination of life with medical assistance **[1]**
2. **Any one from:** Soon after death, the body is washed and wrapped in a linen shroud; prayers of forgiveness are said for the dead and the body is buried in a grave, parallel with Mecca, with the head facing Mecca **[1]**
3. It can be viewed as murder **[1]** and does not allow for forgiveness/rehabilitation. **[1]**
4. 'The Lord gave and the Lord has taken away' **[1]**; Christians believe that God created all life **[1]**; they also believe that only He should end it **[1]**; therefore, many Christians would argue against active euthanasia **[1]**
5.

Agreeing with the statement	Against the statement
It is far cheaper than imprisonment.	The wrong person could be executed.
'An eye for an eye.'	Execution could be seen as murder in itself.
Can bring closure for the family of the victim.	Only God should take life.
Can act as a deterrent to prevent murder.	It could be reserved for only serial murderers.

[Up to 3 marks for reasons in agreement; up to 3 marks in disagreement]

Page 146

1. **Any two from:** The cosmological; the teleological; the moral arguments **[2]**
2. A devout Christian **[1]**, who uses science to argue for God's existence **[1]**
3. A professor who has been described as a committed atheist who argues against the existence of God **[1]** and uses science to support his views **[1]**
4. Many believe we are born with an awareness of what is right or wrong **[1]**; much of UK law is based on the Ten Commandments **[1]**; the ability to judge right from wrong is largely universal **[1]**; this ability can be argued to come from God **[1]**
5. **Any five from:** He developed the teleological argument; the argument is based on the belief that the universe displays design; does a watch suggest design?; can the same not be said for a rock?; the world shows evidence of purpose; the world points towards a creator; God is the Creator, therefore God exists **[5]**

Page 147

1. **Any two from:** Greed, power, money, politics, religion, historical disagreements **[2]**
2. Genesis 4:1–8 **[1]**; Cain and Abel fought over the offerings that they made to God **[1]**
3. Prepare for war **[1]**; rouse the warriors **[1]**
4. Jesus taught that when challenged with conflict we should 'turn the other cheek' **[1]**; therefore, respond with peace to conflict **[1]**; In Matthew 10:34–36, Jesus states families may be divided by His teaching (His words can be seen as a sword) **[1]**; however, many Christians argue that the message that Jesus is bringing is what will divide families, not violence itself **[1]**
5. Developed the Just War Theory in the 13th century **[1]**; its purpose was to lay out how a war could be fairly fought **[1]**; he listed key criteria that should be met and these were further developed to: 1. Have a just cause, 2. Be declared by a lawful authority, 3. Have good intention, 4. Be a last resort. 5. Have a reasonable chance of success. 6. Use proportional force to win, 7. Bring about more good than the harm that it causes **[3]**

Page 148

1. Universal Declaration of Human Rights (UDHR) **[1]**; to protect the basic rights of all people **[1]**
2. A key Buddhist leader **[1]**; has spent much of his life fighting for peace and the rights of Tibetans **[1]**
3. The peacemakers **[1]**; they are children of God **[1]**
4. Pacifism **[1]**; refusing to be part of a war effort in any way **[1]**; conscientious objection **[1]**; refusing to be part of violence in war but supporting the effort in a non-combative role (medic) **[1]**
5. Raise awareness of wars taking place **[1]**; look to protect civilians **[1]**; campaign against suffering caused by war **[1]**; raise funds as a charity **[1]**; focus on the need for diplomacy **[1]**

Page 149

1. Physical punishment **[1]**; e.g. flogging or caning **[1]**
2. **Any two from:** Community service; fines; probation; conditional discharge; absolute discharge; binding over **[2]**
3. The Ten Commandments **[1]**; Exodus 20:1–17 **[1]**
4. **Any four from:** Deterrence – severe punishments to stop a crime being committed; reformation – to change the behaviour of a criminal; protection – prevent further harm being done; reparation – to help an offender to put something back into society; retribution – to see a criminal pay for their actions; vindication – to show that the law is right and must be respected **[4]**
5. **Any five from:** Victims can lose possessions; insurance premiums can then go up, costing others more money; some victims may be injured or lose their lives; victims can feel afraid and insecure; families may struggle to overcome the loss; custodial sentences cost the government money – this could force up the rate of tax **[5]**

Page 150

1. UK – not afford to pay bills or buy food **[1]**; developing world – no clothes, no home, no clean water **[1]**
2. **Any two from:** Debts cancelled; charity work supported; fair price paid for goods **[2]**
3. **Any two from:** Being rich brings complications; it can remove a reliance on God; it can lead to greed; riches on Earth are of little value in the afterlife; the rich should use their wealth to help others **[2]**
4. Money can be used to help others and relieve suffering; money can bring out good in people and there are many examples of wealthy people supporting humanitarian causes **[2]**; money can cause greed and inequality; it can even lead to war; money can take people away from religious values **[2]**

5. Poor people often have few options as they seek to make a better life for themselves and their families [1]; this means they can fall prey to criminals and find themselves used for slavery, drugs trafficking, sham marriages or forced prostitution [1]; unscrupulous employers can take advantage of workers fleeing poverty, by imposing excessively long hours, poor conditions and abuse [1]; people needing money just to get by may be saddled with high interest loans that mean they have to pay back far more than they borrow [1]; there are cases of the poor becoming the targets of unethical brokers in the sale of human organs [1]

Page 151
1. Prejudice is the thought where someone 'pre-judges' [1]; discrimination is when someone acts upon their prejudiced thoughts [1]
2. He fought for equal rights for black people in 1960s USA [1] before being assassinated [1]
3. The separation of the black and white communities, due to race, in South Africa [1] in the 20th century [1]
4. **Any four from:** Racism; sexism; ageism; prejudice based on religion; prejudice based on disability; prejudice based on poverty [4]
5. The Jewish man's own people refused to help him [1]; the rabbi and the Levite were more interested in following the laws [1]; despite being hated by the Jewish nation, the Samaritan stopped to help [1]; the story challenges the prejudice shown by the Jewish people [1]; Jesus stated that all should be treated equally, without prejudice or discrimination [1]

Page 152
1. The basic qualities and opportunities [1] that all people around the world should have available to them [1]
2. The events of the Second World War [1] and the 1947 meeting of the Human Rights Commission [1]
3. 1948 [1]; 30 articles [1]
4. **Any suitable answers, e.g.:** The right to life; the right to free movement; the right to free speech; the right to a fair trial; human rights are protected by law; no slavery; the right to a nationality; no torture; no unfair detainment [4]
5. The UDHR is an international policy [1]; the Human Rights Act (HRA) is a UK Act of Parliament [1]; in many cases, the HRA adds detail to the statutes found in the UDHR [1]; UK courts follow the HRA while following the remit of the European Court of Human Rights [1]; the HRA is amended more frequently, to take into account changes in technology and science [1]

Pages 153–159 Review Questions

Page 153
1. Being able to distinguish between what is right and what is wrong [1]
2. *The God Delusion* [1]
3. The teleological argument [1]
4. **Any two from:** Aquinas argued that the universe must have had a 'cause'; the universe must have been caused by something that was itself uncaused; which he asserted was God; the detail and the sophistication of the universe cannot be accidental; changes in scientific understanding have not undermined the premise of the argument [4]

5.

Agreeing with the statement	Against the statement
Religion can often ignore facts that can be argued disprove God's existence.	In time, science should have the ability to answer the key questions that cannot currently be answered.
Science has advanced greatly but still has gaps in both processes and understanding.	Many would argue that science has already found enough evidence to disprove God's existence.
Even if science could answer conclusively the key questions around the start of life, there would still be room for religious views.	The aim of science is not to disprove God's existence but to continue to build a knowledge base.
Science can also make discoveries that point towards design – laminin in human skin.	Technology holds scientific experimentation back and will eventually allow for more testing.

[Up to 3 marks for reasons in agreement; up to 3 marks in disagreement]

Page 154
1. St Thomas Aquinas [1]
2. A weapon designed to kill in large numbers or to cause great damage, e.g. a nuclear bomb [1]
3. Joel 3:9 [1]
4. War has to be declared [1]; war can be between two or more countries, or between people in the same country (civil war) [1]; conflict may not be violent [1]; troops are much more likely to be engaged during war [1]
5.

Agreeing with the statement	Against the statement
In recent warfare, more civilians die than military personnel.	Sometimes, war is needed to protect people from the rise of an evil regime.
Many conflicts now target the innocent.	The Just War Theory can allow for justification.
Often those who declare wars do not suffer because of the war.	A believer may use their scriptures to justify their actions.
Wars are rarely fought for the benefit of the civilians who could lose their lives.	A war may need to be declared to respond to a conflict – Second World War.

[Up to 3 marks for reasons in agreement; up to 3 marks in disagreement]

Page 155
1. An individual who is against violence of any kind [1]
2. Someone who may support a war effort in a non-violent way [1]
3. To find resolutions that do not lead to war [1]
4. Governments should talk to try to resolve differences [1]; the United Nations can aid these talks [1]; sanctions can be brought against countries unwilling to talk [1]; the UN can be called upon to prevent disputes escalating into war and the international community can work together to prevent a war [1]

5.

Agreeing with the statement	Against the statement
'Do not murder', Exodus 20.	A Christian may feel called to defend others.
Jesus taught that anger was wrong – fighting during war would arguably require anger.	Joining a war effort could stop the spread of an evil power.
The sanctity of life shows life is sacred.	Fighting could also defend their family.
Christians could choose to support in a non-violent way.	'The only thing necessary for evil to prevail is for good men to do nothing', Edmund Burke.

[Up to 3 marks for reasons in agreement; up to 3 marks in disagreement]

Page 156
1. Premeditated murder [1]
2. An act that goes against the will of God [1]
3. Reformation [1]
4. **Any suitable answers, e.g.:** Fine; community service; prison sentence; absolute or conditional discharge; suspended sentence; caution [4]

5.

Agreeing with the statement	Against the statement
Rehabilitating a criminal can help them not to hurt any other person or their property.	It may not be possible to rehabilitate some criminals.
Reducing crime saves the government and the taxpayer money.	The victim should be involved in the justice process and part of the process should focus on their recovery from the crime (restorative justice).
Christians are taught to forgive and rehabilitation is a practical example of this.	A criminal needs to know that their actions were wrong and rehabilitation may not focus enough on the damage and consequences that their actions had.
Part of rehabilitation may include helping the victims of the crimes that have been committed.	Whatever rehabilitation programme is offered, there is no guarantee that the criminal will not reoffend.

[Up to 3 marks for reasons in agreement; up to 3 marks in disagreement]

Page 157
1. **Any two from:** Tornado; hurricane; tsunami; earthquake; volcanic eruption; flooding [1]
2. **Any two from:** Loans; natural disasters; born into poverty; unemployment; criminal activities [2]
3. Raise awareness of poverty in developing countries [1]; prompt wealthier nations to cancel the debt owed to them by poorer countries [1]
4. Each religion teaches its followers that they should help those poorer than themselves [1]; a charity can help in ways that a religious believer might not be able to by themselves [1]; a charity may help to promote the key values of the religion [1]

5.

Agreeing with the statement	Against the statement
Natural disasters and the nature of the global climate make poverty inevitable.	There is sufficient wealth in the world to end poverty; it just needs to be redistributed more fairly.
It is impossible to sustain high rates of economic growth to end poverty.	There is enough will and commitment from people globally to deal with the problem.
Global conflict and war will keep contributing to poverty.	Advancements in technology, e.g. in agriculture and sanitation, will increasingly help.
Politicians will never be able to agree how to share the financial cost of tackling poverty.	Better education and awareness of the problem will eventually lead to solutions being found.

[Up to 3 marks for reasons in agreement; up to 3 marks in disagreement]

Page 158
1. Ageism [1]
2. The principle of humans treating others in the same way as they would wish to be treated [1]
3. Ensure that the problems surrounding it are taught in school [1]; have clear laws regarding prejudice and discrimination [1]; monitor acts of discrimination so that they can be punished [1]; ensure all MPs show equality in their work [1]

4.

Agreeing with the statement	Against the statement
'Love your neighbour as you love yourself.'	Criminals lose the right to equality once sent to prison.
The story of The Good Samaritan.	Muslims are called to support other Muslims first.
Genesis 1 can be used to support the view that we are equal as we are all made 'in God's image'.	Rules in religion can divide people, such as views on homosexuality.
If all were treated equally, the world would most probably be at peace (Galatians 3:28).	During war or conflict, a religious believer may have to defend their country or themselves.

[Up to 3 marks for reasons in agreement; up to 3 marks in disagreement]

Page 159
1. **Any suitable answer, e.g.** Amnesty International [1]
2. The United Nations countries [1]
3. Peter Benenson [1]
4. Christians are called to love each other [1] as they love themselves [1]; to love others requires all to be treated equally [1]; the verse demonstrates the importance of this [1]

5.

Agreeing with the statement	Against the statement
There will always be someone willing to take advantage of another to better themselves.	If the will was great enough, the world could share the wealth more equally.
The greed of one requires another to have less.	Religious believers could help to remove the power of greed.
History and empires have been built upon greed.	Human rights can be respected irrespective of money.
Reversing the pattern of world rule is impossible.	Individuals can help to protect the rights of those around them.

[Up to 3 marks for reasons in agreement; up to 3 marks in disagreement]

Pages 160–161

1. Each day could be a period of time, not 24 hours **[1]**; the Big Bang could have been the start **[1]**; evolution is a theory, not proven fact **[1]**; it is yet to be disproved **[1]**

2. **Any three from:** The Big Bang theory arguably removes the need for God to be the cause; the theory of evolution argues that all life is linked and not individually created; evidence suggests the universe and life in it took millions of years to come about and not, as suggested, six days **[3]**

3. **Any three from:** They are both Abrahamic religions; they share some key prophets; some of the key religious stories are the same; it could be argued that the accounts are based on similar sources **[3]**

4. The biblical account is not meant to be literally true **[1]**; the account allows for details to be omitted **[1]**

Page 162

1. **Any two from:** Issues surrounding prejudice and discrimination; working for peace; unity **[2]**

2. No female Catholic priests **[1]**; only male popes **[1]**; Jesus only chose male disciples **[1]**; the wealth in the Vatican City **[1]**

3. Many wars are fought over issues of race **[1]**; Nazi policy was often developed from discriminatory views **[1]**; equality and equity would bring fairness **[1]**

4. Pacifists believe in promoting peace **[1]**; the image sees different races joined together **[1]**; it helps to symbolise their view of peace through equality and unity **[1]**

Page 163

1. **Any three from:** After the Exodus; wandering in the desert; Moses climbs Mount Sinai; on return, finds Golden Calf; furious; Moses smashes the tablets **[3]**

2. **Any four from:** Shared central beliefs; clear statement of faith; control of morality and behaviour; prohibition of harmful behaviour; protection of the weak; security of person and property **[4]**

3. Do not kill **[1]**; do not steal **[1]**; do not bear false witness **[1]**

4. **Any Commandment supported by two relevant points,**
   e.g. Kill – murder, manslaughter, euthanasia, war; steal – theft, property rights, personal possessions; false witness – lies, false accusations, etc. **[2]**

Page 164

1. **Any four from:** Euthanasia; poverty; care of the elderly; welfare system; discrimination; family responsibility **[4]**

2. **Any three from:** Care of the terminally ill; alternative to hospital care; provides palliative care; alternative to euthanasia; care within the family; end-of-life issues **[3]**

3. **Any three from:** Mercy killing; right to die; murder; suicide; human rights **[3]**

4. **Any two from:** Illness; loneliness; poverty; suffering; fear of death **[2]**

Page 165

1. **Any four from:** Presence of God; importance of holy place; church looks special; family pressures; part of their faith; sacrament; rite of passage **[4]**

2. **Any three from:** Purity; virginity; sex before marriage; marriage of divorcees; living together **[3]**

3. **Any three from:** Holy building; special clothes; wedding vows; involvement of family and friends; presence of God (gods); special food; ring(s) **[3]**

4. **Any two from:** Till death us do part; promises before God; according to God's law; together in *all* circumstances; promise to remain faithful **[2]**

Page 166

1. **Any four from:** Is it humane?; other types of capital punishment are available; alternatives to capital punishment; religious views; moral questions; should humans take the life of others?; sanctity of life **[4]**

2. Retribution; reformation; protection of society; reparation; deterrence; vindication **[3]**

3. **Any three from:** All people commit sin; few commit crime; sin – actions against laws of God; crime – actions against laws of a state; not all sins are crimes – e.g. adultery **[3]**

4. **Any two from:** It is no longer legal; the last execution was in August 1964 by hanging; public opinion varies **[2]**

Page 167

1. **Any three from:** Near-death experiences; ghosts; clairvoyance; religious teaching; resurrection of Jesus; hope in funeral services **[3]**

2. **Any six points from:** Christian – judgement, heaven, hell (and Catholic purgatory); Judaism – heaven, hell, coming of Messiah; Islam – heaven, hell; Sikh – reincarnation **[6]**

3. **Any three from:** Recite the Adhan before death; same gender member of family washes and wraps the body; the body is buried in a grave, parallel with Mecca, head facing Mecca; prayers are said; three days of mourning; cremation is forbidden **[3]**

Page 168

1. **Any three from:** Thank God; pray together; listen to God; to give glory to God; encourage each other in their faith; be close to God; deepen faith; guidance for life **[3]**

2. **Any four from:** Prayer; singing hymns, songs and psalms; listening to a sermon; reading (listening to) scriptures; eating special food; special building **[4]**

3. **Any three from:** Bread – body of Jesus; wine – blood of Jesus; remember the Last Supper; 'do this in remembrance of me'; transubstantiation; sacrifice **[3]**

4. Christians – church; Jews – synagogue; Muslims – mosque; Sikhs – Gurdwara **[2]**

Glossary and Index

Glossary and Index

Collins

GCSE 9-1
Religious Studies

Workbook

Dan Phillips and Rob Phillips

Revision Tips

Rethink Revision

Have you ever taken part in a quiz and thought *'I know this!'* but, despite frantically racking your brain, you just couldn't come up with the answer?

It's very frustrating when this happens but, in a fun situation, it doesn't really matter. However, in your GCSE exams, it will be essential that you can recall the relevant information quickly when you need to.

Most students think that revision is about making sure you **know** stuff. Of course, this is important, but it is also about becoming confident that you can **retain** that *stuff* over time and **recall** it quickly when needed.

Revision That Really Works

Experts have discovered that there are two techniques that help with all of these things and consistently produce better results in exams compared to other revision techniques.

Applying these techniques to your GCSE revision will ensure you get better results in your exams and will have all the relevant knowledge at your fingertips when you start studying for further qualifications, like AS and A Levels, or begin work.

It really isn't rocket science either – you simply need to:

- **test yourself** on each topic as many times as possible
- **leave a gap** between the test sessions.

Three Essential Revision Tips

1. **Use Your Time Wisely**

    - Allow yourself plenty of time.
    - Try to start revising at least six months before your exams – it's more effective and less stressful.
    - Your revision time is precious so use it wisely – using the techniques described on this page will ensure you revise effectively and efficiently and get the best results.
    - Don't waste time re-reading the same information over and over again – it's time-consuming and not effective!

2. **Make a Plan**

    - Identify all the topics you need to revise (this All-in-One Revision & Practice book will help you).
    - Plan at least five sessions for each topic.
    - One hour should be ample time to test yourself on the key ideas for a topic.
    - Spread out the practice sessions for each topic – the optimum time to leave between each session is about one month but, if this isn't possible, just make the gaps as big as realistically possible.

3. **Test Yourself**

    - Methods for testing yourself include: quizzes, practice questions, flashcards, past papers, explaining a topic to someone else, etc.
    - This All-in-One Revision & Practice book provides seven practice opportunities on topics.
    - Don't worry if you get an answer wrong – provided you check what the correct answer is, you are more likely to get the same or similar questions right in future!

Visit our website to download your free flashcards, for more information about the benefits of these techniques, and for further guidance on how to plan ahead and make them work for you.

www.collins.co.uk/collinsGCSErevision

Contents

Mixed Questions

Nature of God

Source A

1 How might Christians describe God? [3]

_____

_____

_____

2 What are the main arguments for the existence of God? [4]

_____

_____

_____

3 What are the main attributes associated with God? [3]

_____

_____

_____

4 What reasons might someone give for not believing in God? [2]

_____

_____

Total Marks _____ / 12

Nuclear War

Source A

1 What type of weapon would cause the explosion shown above? [1]

....

2 What does the abbreviation WMD stand for? [1]

....

3 Why do many people argue against the use of WMDs? [3]

....

....

....

Total Marks .... / 5

Mixed Questions

Miracles

Source A – Mark 6:45–51

[45]Immediately Jesus made his disciples get into the boat and go on ahead of him to Bethsaida, while he dismissed the crowd. [46]After leaving them, he went up on a mountainside to pray.

[47]Later that night, the boat was in the middle of the lake, and he was alone on land. [48]He saw the disciples straining at the oars, because the wind was against them. Shortly before dawn he went out to them, walking on the lake. He was about to pass by them, [49]but when they saw him walking on the lake, they thought he was a ghost. They cried out, [50]because they all saw him and were terrified.

Immediately he spoke to them and said, "Take courage! It is I. Don't be afraid." [51]Then he climbed into the boat with them, and the wind died down.

1 What are the three main types of miracles recorded in the Gospels? [3]

2 How might non-believers explain the accounts of Jesus' miracles? [6]

3 Why might Jesus have performed miracles? [3]

Total Marks _____ / 12

Suffering

Source A

1 Name some of the main causes of suffering. [4]

....

....

....

....

2 Name some of the charities and organisations that work to help those suffering
around the world. [5]

....

....

....

....

....

3 How can individuals help to alleviate suffering? [3]

....

....

....

Total Marks .... / 12

Mixed Questions

Tenakh

Source A

1. Name the three sections of the Tenakh. [3]

2. How do Jews show respect to the Tenakh? [3]

3. Who is allowed to read from the Tenakh in the synagogue during a service? [1]

Total Marks _____ / 7

Discipleship

Source A

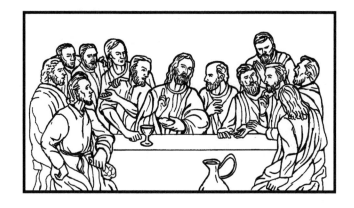

1 What is a disciple? [2]

....

....

2 What characteristics did Jesus expect of His disciples? [5]

....

....

....

....

....

....

3 Who betrayed Jesus? [1]

....

4 Who denied Jesus three times? [1]

....

5 Name three examples of modern-day Christian disciples. [3]

....

....

....

Total Marks .... / 12

Mixed Questions

Mark's Gospel

Source A – Mark 1:1–3

[1]The beginning of the good news about Jesus the Messiah, the Son of God, [2]as it is written in Isaiah the prophet:
"I will send my messenger ahead of you,
who will prepare your way –
[3]a voice of one calling in the wilderness,
'Prepare the way for the Lord,
make straight paths for him.'"

1 Who is being described in verses 2 and 3? [1]

....

2 How many chapters are in Mark's Gospel? [1]

....

3 Which key part of Jesus' life is covered in greater detail in Mark than in the other gospels? [1]

....

4 What evidence is there to suggest that the author of Mark was an eyewitness? [3]

....

....

....

Total Marks .... / 6

Discrimination

Source A

1 What is 'prejudice'? [1]

....

2 Name six types of prejudice. [3]

....

....

....

....

....

3 What is 'discrimination'? [1]

....

4 Why might Christians work against discrimination? [4]

....

....

....

....

Total Marks .... / 9

Mixed Questions

Birth Rites

1 Name the Christian, Jewish and Muslim birth rites. [3]

_____

_____

_____

2 What happens during infant baptism? [5]

_____

_____

_____

_____

_____

3 Why are birth rites important in a believer's life? [4]

_____

_____

_____

_____

Total Marks _____ / 12

Prayer

Source A – Matthew 6:9–13

[9]"This, then, is how you should pray:
'Our Father in heaven,
hallowed be your name,
[10]your kingdom come,
your will be done,
on earth as it is in heaven.
[11]Give us today our daily bread.
[12]And forgive us our debts,
as we also have forgiven our debtors.
[13]And lead us not into temptation,
but deliver us from the evil one.'"

1 Why is this prayer important for Christians? [3]

2 Why do people pray? [5]

3 When and how do Christians pray? [4]

Total Marks _____ / 12

Mixed Questions

The Mosque

Source A

1 What are the main features of the mosque? [5]

_____

_____

_____

_____

2 What are the main features of worship in the mosque? [4]

_____

_____

_____

3 Name three other religious places of worship. [3]

_____

_____

_____

Total Marks _____ / 12

Heaven and Hell

Source A – Revelation 4:1–5

After this I looked, and there before me was a door standing open in heaven. And the voice I had first heard speaking to me like a trumpet said, 'Come up here, and I will show you what must take place after this.' ²At once I was in the Spirit, and there before me was a throne in heaven with someone sitting on it. ³And the one who sat there had the appearance of jasper and ruby. A rainbow that shone like an emerald encircled the throne. ⁴Surrounding the throne were twenty-four other thrones, and seated on them were twenty-four elders. They were dressed in white and had crowns of gold on their heads. ⁵From the throne came flashes of lightning, rumblings and peals of thunder. In front of the throne, seven lamps were blazing. These are the seven spirits of God.

What does each of the following religions teach about heaven and hell?

1 Christianity [4]

2 Judaism [4]

3 Islam [4]

Total Marks .... / 12

Mixed Questions

Design

1 Who used a watch to illustrate the existence of God? [1]

2 How does a watch show design? [3]

3 What do religious believers use as proof of God's existence in the world? [3]

Total Marks _____ / 7

Family

Source A – Exodus 20:12

'Honour your father and mother.'

Source B – Matthew 7:9

'Which of you, if your son asks for bread, would give him a stone?'

1 What do these two verses show? [2]

_____

_____

2 What does it mean to 'honour'? [2]

_____

_____

3 What is the significance of Matthew 7:9? [2]

_____

_____

Total Marks _____ / 6

Collins

GCSE RELIGIOUS STUDIES

Paper 1: Study of Religion
Option 1A – Beliefs, Teachings and Practices: Catholicism

Complete this paper to help you prepare if you have studied Catholicism as your primary religion.

Time allowed: 1 hour

Instructions

- Use black ink or black ball-point pen.
- Answer **all** questions.
- Answer the questions in the space provided.
- Read each question carefully before you start to answer it.
- Try to answer every question. Check your answers if you have time at the end.

Information

- The total mark for this paper is 59.
- The marks for each question are shown in brackets.
- Questions labelled with an **asterisk** (*) are ones where the quality of your written communication will be assessed. *You should take particular care on these questions with your spelling, punctuation and grammar, as well as the use of specialist terminology.*

---

1 Name **three** items that a Catholic may own as part of their faith. **[3 marks]**

2 Give **two** detailed reasons why Catholics value the sacrament of confession. **[4 marks]**

3 Explain **two** reasons why Catholics believe that divorce is wrong.   **[4 marks]**

....

....

....

....

4 Discuss the importance of worship in the life of every Catholic.   **[5 marks]**

....

....

....

....

....

*5 'Catholics should never forget the importance of Jesus' crucifixion.'

Evaluate this statement. In your answer you should:
- refer to Catholic teaching
- give developed arguments to support this statement and a different point of view
- reach a justified conclusion. **[15 marks]**

6 Outline **three** features of the sacrament of Holy Communion. [3 marks]

7 Describe how a Catholic's understanding of the Trinity can aid their everyday life. [4 marks]

8 Where in Mark's Gospel does Jesus direct His followers how to pray? [1 mark]

9 Explain how a Catholic's belief could aid them in making important decisions. [5 marks]

*10 'Each and every Catholic should follow the direction of their church leaders.'

Evaluate this statement. In your answer you should:
- refer to Catholic teaching
- give developed arguments to support this statement and a different point of view
- reach a justified conclusion. **[15 marks]**

Collins

GCSE RELIGIOUS STUDIES

Paper 1: Study of Religion
Option 1B – Beliefs, Teachings and Practices: Christianity

Complete this paper to help you prepare if you have studied Christianity as your primary religion.

Time allowed: 1 hour

Instructions

- Use black ink or black ball-point pen.
- Answer **all** questions.
- Answer the questions in the space provided.
- Read each question carefully before you start to answer it.
- Try to answer every question. Check your answers if you have time at the end.

Information

- The total mark for this paper is 59.
- The marks for each question are shown in brackets.
- Questions labelled with an **asterisk** (*) are ones where the quality of your written communication will be assessed. *You should take particular care on these questions with your spelling, punctuation and grammar, as well as the use of specialist terminology.*

---

1 Name **three** items that a Christian may own as part of their faith.　　　　**[3 marks]**

2 Give **two** detailed reasons why confessing sins is important to Christians.　　　　**[4 marks]**

3 Explain **two** reasons why many Christians believe that divorce is wrong. **[4 marks]**

....

....

....

....

4 Discuss the importance of worship in the life of every Christian. **[5 marks]**

....

....

....

....

GCSE Religious Studies Workbook

*5 'Christians should never forget the importance of Jesus' crucifixion.'

Evaluate this statement. In your answer you should:
- refer to Christian teaching
- give developed arguments to support this statement and a different point of view
- reach a justified conclusion. **[15 marks]**

6 Outline **three** features of the sacrament of Holy Communion. [3 marks]

....

....

....

7 Describe how a Christian's understanding of the Trinity can aid their everyday life. [4 marks]

....

....

....

....

8 Where in Mark's Gospel does Jesus direct His followers how to pray? [1 mark]

....

9 Explain how a Christian's belief could aid them in making important decisions. [5 marks]

....

....

....

....

....

*10 'Each and every Christian should follow the direction of their church leaders.'

Evaluate this statement. In your answer you should:
- refer to Christian teaching
- give developed arguments to support this statement and a different point of view
- reach a justified conclusion.   **[15 marks]**

_____

_____

_____

_____

_____

_____

_____

_____

_____

_____

_____

_____

_____

GCSE RELIGIOUS STUDIES

Paper 2: Study of Second Religion
Option 2A – Beliefs, Teachings and Practices: Islam

Complete this paper to help you prepare if you have studied Islam as your second religion.

Time allowed: 1 hour

Instructions
- Use black ink or black ball-point pen.
- Answer **all** questions.
- Answer the questions in the space provided.
- Read each question carefully before you start to answer it.
- Try to answer every question. Check your answers if you have time at the end.

Information
- The total mark for this paper is 59.
- The marks for each question are shown in brackets.
- Questions labelled with an **asterisk** (*) are ones where the quality of your written communication will be assessed. *You should take particular care on these questions with your spelling, punctuation and grammar, as well as the use of specialist terminology.*

1 Name **three** of the Five Pillars of Islam. **[3 marks]**

....

....

....

2 Give **two** key beliefs that Muslims have with regard to Allah. **[4 marks]**

....

....

....

3 Explain **two** reasons why a Muslim gives money to charity.

[4 marks]

....

....

....

....

4 Discuss the infallibility of the Qur'an as the most important Islamic belief.

[5 marks]

....

....

....

....

....

*5 'Declaring the Shahadah daily is the most important of the Five Pillars.'

Evaluate this statement. In your answer you should:
- refer to Islamic teaching
- give developed arguments to support this statement and a different point of view
- reach a justified conclusion.   **[15 marks]**

6 Give **three** specific routines that only occur during the 30 days of Ramadan. **[3 marks]**

....

....

....

7 Describe **two** ways in which the Qur'an is important to Muslims. **[4 marks]**

....

....

....

....

8 In which one of the following countries does the Hajj take place?

a) Saudi Arabia **b)** Pakistan **c)** India **d)** Iran **[1 mark]**

9 Explain **two** reasons why the Hajj is important for Muslims. **[5 marks]**

....

....

....

....

*10 'It would be heretical for any Muslim to believe that Muhammad was not the most important prophet.'

Evaluate this statement. In your answer you should:
- refer to Islamic teaching
- give developed arguments to support this statement and a different point of view
- reach a justified conclusion.   **[15 marks]**

_____

_____

_____

_____

_____

_____

_____

_____

_____

_____

_____

_____

_____

GCSE RELIGIOUS STUDIES

Paper 2: Study of Second Religion
Option 2B – Beliefs, Teachings and Practices: Judaism

Complete this paper to help you prepare if you have studied Judaism as your second religion.

Time allowed: 1 hour

Instructions

- Use black ink or black ball-point pen.
- Answer **all** questions.
- Answer the questions in the space provided.
- Read each question carefully before you start to answer it.
- Try to answer every question. Check your answers if you have time at the end.

Information

- The total mark for this paper is 59.
- The marks for each question are shown in brackets.
- Questions labelled with an **asterisk** (*) are ones where the quality of your written communication will be assessed. *You should take particular care on these questions with your spelling, punctuation and grammar, as well as the use of specialist terminology.*

---

1 Name **three** characteristics of the Almighty which are described in Genesis 1.   **[3 marks]**

....

....

....

2 Give **two** reasons why only men read the Tenakh from the bimah.   **[4 marks]**

....

....

....

....

3 Explain **two** ways in which the Sabbath is shared. [4 marks]

....

....

....

....

4 Discuss whether the Ten Plagues happened as they are described in the Torah. [5 marks]

....

....

....

....

....

*5 'It makes no sense to believe in the existence of the Almighty.'

Evaluate this statement. In your answer you should:
- refer to Jewish teaching
- give developed arguments to support this statement and a different point of view
- reach a justified conclusion. **[15 marks]**

6 Outline **three** ways in which Jews see Abraham as a role model. **[3 marks]**

7 Describe the importance of the tallit for Jews. **[4 marks]**

8 Which one of the following made the first covenant with the Almighty?

a) Moses   b) Isaac   c) Abraham   d) Noah   **[1 mark]**

9 Explain why circumcision is still important for Jews. **[5 marks]**

*10 'Keeping the Sabbath holy is the most important part of Jewish life.'

Evaluate this statement. In your answer you should:
- refer to Jewish teaching
- give developed arguments to support this statement and a different point of view
- reach a justified conclusion. **[15 marks]**

Collins

GCSE RELIGIOUS STUDIES

Paper 2: Study of Second Religion
Option 2C – Beliefs, Teachings and Practices: Sikhism

Complete this paper to help you prepare if you have studied Sikhism as your second religion.

Time allowed: 1 hour

Instructions

- Use black ink or black ball-point pen.
- Answer **all** questions.
- Answer the questions in the space provided.
- Read each question carefully before you start to answer it.
- Try to answer every question. Check your answers if you have time at the end.

Information

- The total mark for this paper is 59.
- The marks for each question are shown in brackets.
- Questions labelled with an **asterisk** (*****) are ones where the quality of your written communication will be assessed. *You should take particular care on these questions with your spelling, punctuation and grammar, as well as the use of specialist terminology.*

---

1 Outline **three** features of the life of Guru Nanak. **[3 marks]**

2 Explain **two** reasons why the Mool Mantar is important to Sikhs. **[4 marks]**

3 Explain teachings on karma found within Sikhism. [4 marks]

4 Explain **two** reasons why the Five Ks are significant symbols for Sikhs. [5 marks]

*5 'The work of Guru Gobind Singh is greater than that of any other Guru.'

Evaluate this statement. In your answer you should:
- refer to Sikh teaching
- give developed arguments to support this statement and a different point of view
- reach a justified conclusion.   **[15 marks]**

6 Outline **three** features of the Sikh Naming Ceremony.   [3 marks]

....

....

....

7 Describe the layout of the main worship area in a Gurdwara and its purpose.   [4 marks]

....

....

....

....

8 Which one of the following was the final Sikh Guru?

a) Guru Nanak **b)** Guru Gobind Singh **c)** Guru Angad **d)** Guru Arjan   [1 mark]

9 Explain why attending the Gurdwara every week is important for Sikhs.   [5 marks]

....

....

....

....

....

*10 'All male Sikhs should become part of the Khalsa brotherhood.'

Evaluate this statement. In your answer you should:
- refer to Sikh teaching
- give developed arguments to support this statement and a different point of view
- reach a justified conclusion. **[15 marks]**

....

....

....

....

....

....

....

....

....

....

....

....

....

Collins

GCSE RELIGIOUS STUDIES

Paper 3: Textual Study
Option 3A – Mark's Gospel

Complete this paper to help you prepare if you have studied Mark's Gospel.

Time allowed: 1 hour

Instructions

- Use black ink or black ball-point pen.
- Answer **all** questions.
- Answer the questions in the space provided.
- Read each question carefully before you start to answer it.
- Try to answer every question. Check your answers if you have time at the end.

Information

- The total mark for this paper is 51.
- The marks for each question are shown in brackets.
- Questions labelled with an **asterisk** (*) are ones where the quality of your written communication will be assessed. *You should take particular care on these questions with your spelling, punctuation and grammar, as well as the use of specialist terminology.*

---

1 Which one of the following was the name of the first disciple called by Jesus?

   a) Simon   **b)** Thomas   **c)** John   **d)** Judas   **[1 mark]**

2 Give **two** reasons why Jesus performing miracles on the Sabbath was controversial.   **[2 marks]**

3 Explain **two** reasons how the feeding of the 5000 and the 4000 can prove Jesus was God. **[4 marks]**

....

....

....

....

....

4 Explain **two** illustrations Jesus used to teach about the Kingdom of God. **[5 marks]**

....

....

....

....

....

....

5 'Jesus was rejected because He challenged the authority of the Pharisees.'

Evaluate this statement. In your answer you:
- should give reasoned arguments in support of this statement
- should give reasoned arguments to support a different point of view
- should refer to Mark's Gospel in your answer
- may refer to non-religious arguments
- should reach a justified conclusion. **[12 marks]**

....

....

....

....

....

....

6 In which one of the following chapters is Jesus' crucifixion recorded?

a) 13   **b)** 14   **c)** 15   **d)** 16   [1 mark]

7 Give **two** reasons why Jesus chose only male disciples.   [2 marks]

8 Give **two** detailed reasons why Jesus called fishermen as His first disciples.   [4 marks]

9 Explain **two** reasons why Jesus told the Parable of the Sower. [5 marks]

....

....

....

....

....

....

*10 'The disciples initially doubting that Jesus had risen from the dead can encourage Christians today.'

Evaluate this statement. In your answer you:
- should give reasoned arguments in support of this statement
- should give reasoned arguments to support a different point of view
- should refer to Mark's Gospel in your answer
- should reach a justified conclusion. [15 marks]

....

....

....

....

....

....

....

....

....

....

....

Collins

GCSE RELIGIOUS STUDIES

Paper 3: Textual Study
Option 3B – The Qur'an

Complete this paper to help you prepare if you have studied the Qur'an.

Time allowed: 1 hour

Instructions

- Use black ink or black ball-point pen.
- Answer **all** questions.
- Answer the questions in the space provided.
- Read each question carefully before you start to answer it.
- Try to answer every question. Check your answers if you have time at the end.

Information

- The total mark for this paper is 51.
- The marks for each question are shown in brackets.
- Questions labelled with an **asterisk** (*) are ones where the quality of your written communication will be assessed. *You should take particular care on these questions with your spelling, punctuation and grammar, as well as the use of specialist terminology.*

---

1 Which one of the following languages was the Qur'an originally recorded in?

   a) Arabic   **b)** English   **c)** Aramic   **d)** Sanskrit   **[1 mark]**

2 How is the Qur'an stored in the home when not being read?   **[2 marks]**

----

3 Explain **two** ways in which the teachings in the Qur'an about charity will affect the life of a Muslim today.   [4 marks]

....

....

....

....

4 Explain **two** reasons why it is still important for a Muslim to learn Arabic today.   [5 marks]

....

....

....

....

....

....

5 'Allah chose to send numerous prophets before Muhammad to ensure that people were ready to receive the Qur'an.'

Evaluate this statement. In your answer you:
- should give reasoned arguments in support of this statement
- should give reasoned arguments to support a different point of view
- should refer to the Qur'an in your answer
- may refer to non-religious arguments
- should reach a justified conclusion.   [12 marks]

....

....

....

....

....

....

....

....

....

....

....

....

6 Which of the following names is given to denote a chapter in the Qur'an?

a) Surah   **b)** Ayat   **c)** Section   **d)** Division   **[1 mark]**

7 Outline the works of the prophet Nuh.   **[2 marks]**

....

....

8 Explain **two** ways in which Isa is important for Muslims.   **[4 marks]**

....

....

....

....

9 Explain **two** reasons why Muhammad is seen to be a good role model for Muslims today.   **[5 marks]**

*10 'Allah bestows blessings on those who believe in Him and follow Him.'

Evaluate this statement. In your answer you:
- should give reasoned arguments in support of this statement
- should give reasoned arguments to support a different point of view
- should refer to the Qur'an in your answer
- should reach a justified conclusion.   **[15 marks]**

GCSE RELIGIOUS STUDIES

Paper 4: Religion, Philosophy and Ethics
Option 4A – Relationships and Family

Complete this paper to help you prepare if you have studied Relationships and Family as a Religion, Philosophy and Ethics topic.

Time allowed: 45 minutes

Instructions

- Use black ink or black ball-point pen.
- Answer **all** questions.
- Answer the questions in the space provided.
- Read each question carefully before you start to answer it.
- Try to answer every question. Check your answers if you have time at the end.

Information

- The total mark for this paper is 27.
- The marks for each question are shown in brackets.
- Questions labelled with an **asterisk** (*) are ones where the quality of your written communication will be assessed. *You should take particular care on these questions with your spelling, punctuation and grammar, as well as the use of specialist terminology.*

---

1 Which one of the following is the name given to the religious and legal union between a man and woman?

    a) Cohabitation   **b)** Marriage   **c)** Civil partnership   **d)** Relationship   **[1 mark]**

2 Give **two** reasons why some families practise arranged marriages.   **[2 marks]**

3 Explain why marriage vows are important in any religion.   **[4 marks]**

....

....

....

....

4 Explain **two** reasons why people get married.   **[5 marks]**

....

....

....

....

....

*5 'Marriage is an outdated ritual and is no longer as important as it once was.'

Evaluate this statement. In your answer you:
- should give reasoned arguments in support of this statement
- should give reasoned arguments to support a different point of view
- may refer to non-religious arguments
- should reach a justified conclusion. **[15 marks]**

_____

_____

_____

_____

_____

_____

_____

_____

_____

_____

_____

_____

_____

_____

Collins

GCSE RELIGIOUS STUDIES

Paper 4: Religion, Philosophy and Ethics
Option 4B – Existence of God

Complete this paper to help you prepare if you have studied Existence of God as a Religion, Philosophy and Ethics topic.

Time allowed: 45 minutes

Instructions

- Use black ink or black ball-point pen.
- Answer **all** questions.
- Answer the questions in the space provided.
- Read each question carefully before you start to answer it.
- Try to answer every question. Check your answers if you have time at the end.

Information

- The total mark for this paper is 27.
- The marks for each question are shown in brackets.
- Questions labelled with an **asterisk** (*) are ones where the quality of your written communication will be assessed. *You should take particular care on these questions with your spelling, punctuation and grammar, as well as the use of specialist terminology.*

---

1 Which one of the following characteristics attributes the quality of goodness to the Christian God?

   a) Omnipresent **b)** Omniscient **c)** Omnibenevolent **d)** Omnipotent   **[1 mark]**

2 Give **two** reasons why people choose to believe in God.   **[2 marks]**

3 Explain **two** reasons why some may argue that God's existence can never be proven. **[4 marks]**

4 Explain **two** teachings Christians can find evidence for in the book of Revelation. **[5 marks]**

*5 'Having so many beliefs about who God may be weakens the argument that any god exists.'

Evaluate this statement. In your answer you:
- should give reasoned arguments in support of this statement
- should give reasoned arguments to support a different point of view
- may refer to non-religious arguments
- should reach a justified conclusion. **[15 marks]**

GCSE RELIGIOUS STUDIES

Paper 4: Religion, Philosophy and Ethics
Option 4C – Peace and Conflict

Complete this paper to help you prepare if you have studied Peace and Conflict as a Religion, Philosophy and Ethics topic.

Time allowed: 45 minutes

Instructions

- Use black ink or black ball-point pen.
- Answer **all** questions.
- Answer the questions in the space provided.
- Read each question carefully before you start to answer it.
- Try to answer every question. Check your answers if you have time at the end.

Information

- The total mark for this paper is 27.
- The marks for each question are shown in brackets.
- Questions labelled with an **asterisk** (*) are ones where the quality of your written communication will be assessed. *You should take particular care on these questions with your spelling, punctuation and grammar, as well as the use of specialist terminology.*

---

1 How many human rights are included in the Universal Declaration?

a) 20 **b)** 25 **c)** 30 **d)** 35 [1 mark]

2 Give **two** reasons why a Christian may argue against fighting during war. [2 marks]

3 Explain **two** reasons why a pacifist promotes diplomacy. **[4 marks]**

....

....

....

....

4 Explain **two** ways in which religion can cause conflict. **[5 marks]**

....

....

....

....

....

*5 'Nuclear weapon arsenals should be maintained to deter war around the world.'

Evaluate this statement. In your answer you:
- should give reasoned arguments in support of this statement
- should give reasoned arguments to support a different point of view
- may refer to non-religious arguments
- should reach a justified conclusion.

[15 marks]

Collins

GCSE RELIGIOUS STUDIES

Paper 4: Religion, Philosophy and Ethics
Option 4D – Crime and Punishment

Complete this paper to help you prepare if you have studied Crime and Punishment as a Religion, Philosophy and Ethics topic.

Time allowed: 45 minutes

Instructions

- Use black ink or black ball-point pen.
- Answer **all** questions.
- Answer the questions in the space provided.
- Read each question carefully before you start to answer it.
- Try to answer every question. Check your answers if you have time at the end.

Information

- The total mark for this paper is 27.
- The marks for each question are shown in brackets.
- Questions labelled with an **asterisk** (*) are ones where the quality of your written communication will be assessed. *You should take particular care on these questions with your spelling, punctuation and grammar, as well as the use of specialist terminology.*

---

1 Which one of the following countries serves the most death penalties each year?

a) USA b) China c) Iraq d) Cuba **[1 mark]**

2 Give **two** reasons why crimes have to be punished. **[2 marks]**

3 Explain **two** benefits from punishing with the aim to reform an individual. **[4 marks]**

_____

_____

_____

_____

4 Explain **two** reasons why the death penalty is no longer served in the UK. **[5 marks]**

_____

_____

_____

_____

_____

*5 'All punishments should primarily aim to fulfil the wishes of the crime's victim(s).'

Evaluate this statement. In your answer you:
- should give reasoned arguments in support of this statement
- should give reasoned arguments to support a different point of view
- may refer to non-religious arguments
- should reach a justified conclusion.

[15 marks]

Collins

GCSE RELIGIOUS STUDIES

Paper 4: Religion, Philosophy and Ethics
Option 4E – Human Rights and Social Justice

Complete this paper to help you prepare if you have studied Human Rights and Social Justice as a Religion, Philosophy and Ethics topic.

Time allowed: 45 minutes

Instructions

- Use black ink or black ball-point pen.
- Answer **all** questions.
- Answer the questions in the space provided.
- Read each question carefully before you start to answer it.
- Try to answer every question. Check your answers if you have time at the end.

Information

- The total mark for this paper is 27.
- The marks for each question are shown in brackets.
- Questions labelled with an **asterisk** (*) are ones where the quality of your written communication will be assessed. *You should take particular care on these questions with your spelling, punctuation and grammar, as well as the use of specialist terminology.*

---

1 Which one of the following is a form of discrimination?

    a) Bullying   **b)** Racism   **c)** Sexism   **d)** Ageism   **[1 mark]**

2 Give **two** reasons why a religious believer should not discriminate against others. **[2 marks]**

3 Explain **two** reasons why Martin Luther King Jr stood against prejudice. [4 marks]

_____

_____

_____

_____

4 Explain **two** ways in which UK law aims to protect human rights. [5 marks]

_____

_____

_____

_____

_____

_____

*5 'We should always treat people equally.'

Evaluate this statement. In your answer you:
- should give reasoned arguments in support of this statement
- should give reasoned arguments to support a different point of view
- may refer to non-religious arguments
- should reach a justified conclusion.   **[15 marks]**

Notes

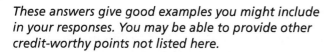

Answers

These answers give good examples you might include in your responses. You may be able to provide other credit-worthy points not listed here.

Pages 188–201 Mixed Questions

Page 188

1. **Any three from:** Old man with beard; all-loving; all-powerful; eternal power; like Jesus; a spirit; world soul; Father; Trinity; friend **[3]**
2. **Any four from:** Ontological; cosmological; from design; from experience; teleological; moral **[4]**
3. **Any four from:** Omnipotent; omniscient; omnipresent; omnibenevolent; eternal **[3]**
4. **Any two from:** There is too much suffering in the world; science provides too many reasons for God to exist; they have never experienced Him; religions contradict each other **[2]**

Page 189

1. A nuclear bomb **[1]**
2. Weapons of mass destruction **[1]**
3. **Any three from:** They can be used to target civilians; they are intended to kill large numbers of people; they can cause long-term health problems, for future generations; they can cause long-term environmental damage; they could never be used in a Just War **[3]**

Page 190

1. Healing miracles and exorcisms **[1]**; nature miracles **[1]**; resurrections **[1]**
2. **Any six from:** Natural phenomena; superstition; psychosomatic illnesses; mind over matter; legends and myths; exaggeration; faulty memories; hero worship; Jesus was a medic, ahead of his time **[6]**
3. **Any three from:** Response to faith; encourage faith; compassion; demonstrate the power of God; show who he was (Messianic miracles); show he had the ability to forgive sins **[3]**

Page 191

1. **Any four from:** Famine; war; natural disasters; disease; selfishness; abuse of power **[4]**
2. **Any five from:** Tearfund; Oxfam; CAFOD; Christian Aid; Red Cross; Red Crescent; Disasters Emergency Committee (DEC); any other appropriate aid organisation **[5]**
3. **Any three from:** Fundraising; personal giving; volunteering; pressure groups; raising awareness; education **[3]**

Page 192

1. The Torah **[1]**; the Nevi'im **[1]**; the Ketuvim **[1]**
2. **Any three from:** It is handwritten; it is only produced in scroll form for use in the synagogue; a yad has to be used when reading as words are never touched; when copied nothing is altered; kept in special place; richly decorated; when damaged, it is buried not destroyed **[3]**
3. Any male who has passed through their Bar Mitzvah **[1]**

Page 193

1. **Any two from:** Follower; learner; devotee; student **[2]**
2. **Any five from:** Child-like; dependent; sacrificial; faithful; dedicated; humble; servant of all **[5]**
3. Judas Iscariot **[1]**
4. Simon Peter **[1]**
5. **Any three from:** Mother Teresa; Martin Luther King; Dietrich Bonhoeffer; Billy Graham; Corrie Ten Boom; Jackie Pullinger; any other appropriate individuals **[3]**

Page 194

1. John the Baptist **[1]**
2. 16 **[1]**
3. The Passion of Christ (the last week of Jesus' life) **[1]**
4. **Any three from:** The way in which he refers to himself; the writing style of the Gospel; the focus upon the Passion; some of the details included **[3]**

Page 195

1. **Any one from:** Deciding in advance of the evidence; forming opinions without evidence, often based on stereotypes; to judge before knowing an individual **[1]**
2. **Any six from:** Age; race; gender; disability; sexual orientation; social status; poverty; political views; religion **[3]**
3. Acting on prejudice **[1]**
4. **Any four from:** All equal in sight of God; all made in God's image; love neighbour; love enemy; example of Jesus; parable of the Good Samaritan; Galatians 3:28 **[4]**

Page 196

1. Christian – Baptism or Dedication **[1]**; Jewish – Brit Milah **[1]**; Muslim – Aqeeqah (is one part of Islamic customs) **[1]**
2. **Any five from:** Prayers; promises by parents and godparents; water on head of baby; cleansing and rebirth; sign of cross; lighted candle – darkness to light; naming of the child **[5]**
3. **Any four from:** Thanksgiving for birth; dedication to God; welcome into family of faith; start of faith journey; collective responsibility for religious education **[4]**

Page 197

1. **Any three from:** Taught by Jesus; pattern for prayer; learned and repeated; actual words of Jesus **[3]**
2. **Any five from:** To say thank you; praise; petition; adoration; get close to God; meditation; listen to God; to confess sin **[5]**

Answers

3. **Any four from:** In private; in church; daily; in small groups; silently; set prayers; out loud; extemporary (unscripted) **[4]**

Page 198

1. **Any five from:** Minaret; dome; wash room; prayer hall; mihrab; mimbar; shoe rack; prayer mats **[5]**
2. **Any four from:** Call to prayer; prayer five times a day; Friday prayers; optional for women; ritual washing (wudu); face Mecca; imam; sermon **[4]**
3. Christians – church **[1]**; Jews – synagogue **[1]**; Sikhs – Gurdwara **[1]**

Page 199

1. Judgement
   Heaven: Where God is; eternal; result of salvation; many believe it is a physical place while others believe it is spiritual only
   Hell: Where God is not; eternal; result of sin; place of punishment; place created for Lucifer and fallen angels
   (For Catholics there is also purgatory.)
   (Any two from each up to a maximum of 4)
2. Judgement
   Heaven: eternity with God; place of celebration
   Hell: eternity without God; punishment
   Sheol: spirits awaiting the Messiah
   Limbo: judgement will only occur, and Sheol be no more, after the Messiah has come.
   (Any two from each up to a maximum of 4)
3. Judgement
   Paradise: Jannah; physical and spiritual pleasure; beautiful mansions; food and drink; virgins
   Hell: Jahannam; seven levels of physical and spiritual suffering; cauldron of burning pitch
   (Any two from each up to a maximum of 4)

Page 200

1. William Paley **[1]**
2. The mechanism works **[1]**; it cannot have happened by chance **[1]**; it has a purpose **[1]**
3. **Any three from:** The beauty of nature; the awe and wonder of human life; the molecular structure of items as simple as rocks; the laws of nature; the patterns and systems occurring naturally in the world **[3]**

Page 201

1. Parents and children have their own responsibilities **[1]**; the Bible defines the roles of both children and parents **[1]**
2. To follow instruction **[1]**; to show respect **[1]**
3. **Any two from:** Parents should provide for their children/they should not deny their children food; parents should want to protect their children; the nature of God as a caring Father **[2]**

PRACTICE EXAM PAPERS

Note: Your exam board may use a different mark scheme to the one which follows.

For questions worth 15 marks, use the following mark scheme to assess your answers:

- **12 of the marks are for the quality of your evaluation.**
- **3 of the marks are for your spelling, punctuation and grammar and use of specialist terminology (SPaG).**

1–3 marks for:
- identifying information/issues and making superficial connections among a limited range of elements in the question, underpinned by isolated elements of understanding of religion and belief.
- judgements that are supported by generic arguments to produce a conclusion that is not fully justified.

4–6 marks for:
- making superficial connections among many, but not all, of the elements in the question, underpinned by a limited understanding of religion and belief.
- making judgements of a limited range of elements in the question. Judgements are supported by an attempt to appraise evidence, much of which may be superficial, leading to a conclusion that is not fully justified.

7–9 marks for:
- deconstructing religious information/issues, leading to coherent and logical chains of reasoning that consider different viewpoints. These are underpinned by an accurate understanding of religion and belief. Connections are made among many, but not all, of the elements in the question.
- constructing coherent and reasoned judgements of many, but not all, of the elements in the question. Judgements are supported by the appraisal of evidence, some of which may be superficial, leading to a partially justified conclusion.

10–12 marks for:
- critically deconstructing religious information/issues, leading to coherent and logical chains of reasoning that consider different viewpoints. These are underpinned by a sustained, accurate and thorough understanding of religion and belief. Connections are made among the full range of elements in the question.
- constructing coherent and reasoned judgements of the full range of elements in the question. Judgements are fully supported by the comprehensive appraisal of evidence, leading to a fully justified conclusion.

SPaG

0 marks for:
- writing nothing
- a response that does not relate to the question.
- errors in spelling, punctuation and grammar that severely hinder meaning.

1 mark for:
- spelling and punctuating with reasonable accuracy.
- using rules of grammar with some control of meaning and any errors do not significantly hinder meaning overall.
- a limited range of specialist terms used as appropriate.

2 marks for:
- spelling and punctuating with considerable accuracy.
- using rules of grammar with general control of meaning overall.
- using a good range of specialist terms as appropriate.

3 marks for:
- spelling and punctuating with consistent accuracy.
- using rules of grammar with effective control of meaning overall.
- using a wide range of specialist terms as appropriate.

PAPER 1A – STUDY OF RELIGION: BELIEFS, TEACHINGS AND PRACTICES: CATHOLICISM

Pages 202–206

1 A bible; a set of Rosary beads; a copy of the Catechism; a crucifix.
2 Allows confession of sin – penance can then be served; allows freedom from sins committed and forgiveness for them.
3 Marriage vows are made in church before God; the couple vow to be together for life; the marriage contract is a legally binding document; if God has made a couple 'one', that should not be separated; would be damaging to each person.
4 Following the liturgy can bring a sense of peace; examples of worship can be seen throughout the Bible; helping others may be of greater importance; following biblical principles; Jesus prayed; allows closeness with God; creates a sense of community and fellowship; can share the sacrament of Holy Communion; songs allow for praise and thankfulness to be expressed; can bring glory to God.
5 Allows Catholics to feel assured about what will happen to them in the afterlife; it sets Jesus apart from the rest of creation; the crucifixion precedes the importance of the resurrection; reveals the sacrifice of Christ; allows passage into heaven; sins can be forgiven; can be seen in belief statements such as the Nicene Creed; the role and importance of confession is elevated; the greatest commandments teaching Catholics how to live should be at the forefront of their mind.
6 Sharing bread and wine; reciting words spoken at the Last Supper; remember Jesus' sacrifice; confess sins; focus on the forgiveness of His resurrection.
7 Explaining what the Trinity is; describing the nature of God; knowing God can aid their prayer and worship; understanding the relationship within the Trinity can help them in their relationship with God; a further mark for explanation of each point, and any other valid points can earn a mark.
8 Mark 5; Mark 9; Mark 11; Mark 13.
9 Read the Bible – look for guidance from the past experiences of others, study verses about similar situations, ask God to speak to them through His Word; pray to God – ask for answers and guidance; speak to other Catholics – ask them to study scripture and to pray on their behalf; worship in church – allowing quiet meditation for God to speak to them; consult their priest – ask for his advice and guidance.
10 Catholics recognise the role of leadership from biblical times; they follow the model of Peter being essentially the first Pope; each church has a hierarchy that then feeds into the larger Church; the Pope – he leads the entire Church from the Vatican, and guides the hierarchy that exists there; his role is to provide guidance in the modern world and help shape teachings from the root of the Bible; the Church promotes the value of the priest through confession and his ability to intercede for the Catholic person; the role of saints is emphasised, with their historical leadership valued and promoted.

PAPER 1B – STUDY OF RELIGION: BELIEFS, TEACHINGS AND PRACTICES: CHRISTIANITY

Pages 207–211

1 A bible; an Icthus symbol; a cross.
2 Allows them to be drawn closer to God; allows freedom from sins that have been committed and forgiveness for them; enables them to show remorse and learn from their mistakes; allows them to enter into heaven in the next life.
3 Marriage vows are made in church before God; the couple vow to be together for life; the marriage contract is a legally binding document.
4 Following the liturgy can bring a sense of peace; examples of worship can be seen throughout the Bible; helping others may be of greater importance; following biblical principles; Jesus prayed; allows closeness with God; creates a sense of community and fellowship; can share the sacrament of Holy Communion; songs allow for praise and thankfulness to be expressed; meeting with others for worship strengthens and supports faith; it can help a believer bring glory to God, which is what He intended, whether musical worship or worship through serving others.
5 Allows Christians to feel assured about what will happen to them in the afterlife; sets Jesus apart from the rest of creation; the crucifixion

Answers

precedes the importance of the resurrection; reveals the sacrifice of Christ; Jesus knew what is was to experience suffering; allows passage into heaven; sins can be forgiven; can be seen in belief statements such as the Nicene Creed; the role and importance of confession is elevated.

6   Sharing bread and wine; reciting words spoken at the Last Supper; remember Jesus' sacrifice; confess sins; focus on the forgiveness of His resurrection.

7   Explaining what the Trinity is; describing the nature of God; knowing God can aid their prayer and worship; a further mark for explanation of each point, and any other valid points can earn a mark.

8   Mark 5; Mark 9; Mark 11; Mark 13.

9   Read the Bible – look for guidance from the past experiences of others, study verses about similar situations, ask God to speak to them through His Word; pray to God – ask for answers and guidance; speak to other Christians – ask them to study scripture and to pray on their behalf; worship in church – allowing quiet meditation for God to speak to them; consult their priest/minister – ask for his advice and guidance.

10 Christians recognise the role of leadership from biblical times; the authority and position of leaders is respected in church leadership models; the biblical accounts of the disciples and the early Church support leadership; the role of saints is emphasised, with their historical leadership valued and promoted; historically, priests were able to intercede with God on behalf of Christians; Paul speaks of the Church being 'the body of Christ'; all Christians have their role to play and may challenge leadership; leaders are only human and are not infallible.

PAPER 2A – STUDY OF SECOND RELIGION: BELIEFS, TEACHINGS AND PRACTICES: ISLAM

Pages 212–216

1   Zakah; Shahadah; Hajj; Salah; Sawm.

2   Allah is the only God – there is no other like Him; He is just and merciful and treats all as they should be treated.

3   They are instructed to in the Qur'an, so are following the teachings of Allah; the 2.5% of their income goes towards helping Muslims who are in a worse financial position.

4   Is at the heart of the belief about the importance of Muhammad; sets the Qur'an apart from all other holy scriptures; reveals the nature of trust that Allah had in Muhammad; shows how Allah can speak to humanity; the Qur'an underlines the faithfulness of Muhammad's followers; Muslims could argue that the Five Pillars are more important; the declaration of the Shahadah could also have greater significance.

5   All Muslims should declare the greatness of Allah every day; they should remind themselves of His role as the only God; this declaration can serve as an example to those around them; glorifying Allah will lead each believer to a sense of spirituality; however, Zakah helps the poor around them; it could bring the poor to a place to help others; journeying on the Hajj allows a Muslim to experience moments similar to those Muhammad would have experienced in his life; praying five times a day is very closely linked to the Shahadah; fasting during Ramadan shows commitment to Islam and also allows for greater time to be spent in prayer and service.

6   Muslims will only eat before sunrise and after sunset; they will only eat simple foods during these times; extra time is given over to prayer and serving others.

7   It is the spoken word of Allah given to Muhammad for all Muslims; the Qur'an allows Muslims to find closeness and a connection with Allah.

8   a) Saudi Arabia

9   Hajj allows a Muslim to join with many other Muslims and share in religious rituals with them; the pilgrimage also allows them to follow in the footsteps and experiences of Muhammad; it is one of the Five Pillars.

10 Muhammad is second only to Allah; Muslims believe that Allah chose Muhammad above all others; Muhammad was chosen to receive the Qur'an; however, Muhammad is lesser than Allah and should never be seen as being equal; Muslims believe that he was the last of the prophets and that he brought the greatest revelations from Allah; Muslims believe that Allah spoke directly to Muhammad and also through the angel Jibril; through the power of his teaching, Muhammad gained many followers; the speed at which he amassed his followers allowed him to create a strong army; Muhammad's army was then blessed by Allah and defeated Mecca to found the nation of Islam; some would argue Isa is equal to Muhammad; they could argue that the two prophets were given different callings.

PAPER 2B – STUDY OF SECOND RELIGION: BELIEFS, TEACHINGS AND PRACTICES: JUDAISM

Pages 217–221

1   He has always been; He is the Creator of all; He is without physical form as He moved over the waters.

2   The leading figures in Judaism were all male – they continue this tradition; males are taught how to read the Tenakh with much greater rigour; men and women have different roles to play – leadership in the synagogue is a male responsibility.

3   In the home as a family; the table is set; the mother lights the candle; wine and two loaves of challah bread are shared.

4 Some are explainable by science; disease could easily have wiped out livestock; changes in climate and water temperature could have been responsible for some of the plagues associated with insects; the death of the first born is the most difficult to explain; disease could have been genetic to only the Egyptians but would not have only happened on one night; the timescale and order of the plagues would be difficult to explain, even today.

5 Suffering affects millions around the world on a daily basis; greed and selfishness are two major weaknesses in humanity; why does the Almighty no longer intervene as He did in scripture? Does this raise questions about the validity of scripture? Stories such as creation can now largely be explained by science; the presence of the Almighty can still be seen today in examples such as the beauty of nature and in newborn babies; people still come to faith despite what they see in the world around them; science has still been unable to disprove the existence of the Almighty.

6 Trusted in the Almighty for a son, despite his age; was willing to sacrifice his son for the Almighty; his trust in the Almighty was visible in that he put Him above all else, leaving his family and home; was part of the covenant of circumcision with the Almighty.

7 It is a symbol of faith; it reminds them of the 613 laws they are to follow; often received as a gift after Bar/Bat Mitzvah.

8 c) Abraham

9 It remembers the covenant between Abraham and the Almighty; it continues this declaration of faith; it separates them from other faiths; the ceremony brings the family together; circumcision brings the boy into Judaism and helps him to grow in the faith; shows a lifelong commitment to the faith; it shows a physical declaration of an inner spirituality.

10 One of the Ten Sayings; allows time for worship and a break from work; brings the family together; is a weekly reminder of the history of the faith; provides a focused time of prayer and worship in the house; keeping the 613 laws may be seen as being more important; attending the synagogue for worship or learning scriptures could have greater value; that certain acts (such as saving life on the Sabbath) are permitted, suggests some actions are more important; seeking to spend personal time in devotion could bring a Jew closer to the Almighty; living their life to express their devotion to the Almighty could help to influence others.

PAPER 2C – STUDY OF SECOND RELIGION: BELIEFS, TEACHINGS AND PRACTICES: SIKHISM

Pages 222–226

1 Grew up in a Hindu family; was taught by a Muslim teacher; spent three days when 30 being spoken to by Naam before beginning Sikhism.

2 It declares that there is only one God and is said every day; it sets out the nature of Naam and it appears at the start of every section of the Guru Granth Sahib.

3 Sikhs believe in reincarnation, the rebirth of the soul; in this life and the next, Sikhs believe deeds, both good and bad, are repaid in equal measure; the Guru Granth Sahib contains teachings on karma.

4 Guru Gobind Singh created the Khalsa brotherhood and the Five Ks are symbols of this; it allowed Sikhs to defend their religion; it stopped the faith from being wiped out by the surrounding Hindus and Muslims; the Five Ks provided a basic but effective defensive armour; without them, Sikhism may not exist today.

5 Guru Nanak was obviously the founder; without him, it could be argued that Sikhism would have never come into existence; others could argue that Naam would have been revealed to another; Guru Gobind Singh modelled sacrifice; he showed the religion how to defend itself; he equipped them with the means to survive; he also declared there would be no further human Gurus after him; it could be argued that he has created a far greater legacy; he oversaw the completion of the Guru Granth Sahib; in addition, he also showed Sikhs how to use the book as a guide.

6 The child is given their first name after the Guru Granth Sahib is used to determine the first letter of their name, along with Singh for a boy or Kaur for a girl; prayers are whispered over the baby and Kara Parshad is shared.

7 An open room without chairs; a division in the room to separate men and women; a raised area (lectern) for the Guru Granth Sahib to be read from, which allows all to sit below the book to show respect.

8 b) Guru Gobind Singh

9 Sikhs can hear the Guru Granth Sahib being read; hearing allows opportunity for them to receive guidance or teaching; they can spend time in focused meditation; time can be spent sharing food in the langar hall; they could also spend time serving others there; whilst doing this, they can share their faith with non-believers; being with other Sikhs can support them and build their faith.

10 Many feel called to set an example; wearing the Five Ks sets them apart; it is a lifelong commitment; the rules of being a part of the brotherhood are stricter than not being a part of it; if any rules are broken, the Sikh has to appear before his elders, where he may be given tasks of repentance to complete before his re-acceptance; some would argue that it is difficult to follow in a modern world; Sikhs may struggle to maintain the commitment in their daily life; others may argue that the brotherhood is not sexist but separates where it should unify.

PAPER 3A – TEXTUAL STUDY: MARK'S GOSPEL

Pages 227–230

1 a) Simon

2   Many saw it as work and therefore against the teachings of the Torah; the Pharisees believed Him to be heretical and guilty of blasphemy – these acts added to that claim.

3   Feeding these numbers of people was obviously outside of the laws of nature; for those present it showed something divine about Jesus; His disciples saw Jesus' power over nature.

4   The Parable of the Sower demonstrates how many will hear the Word of God but will respond to it in different ways; the Parable of the Lamp is used to illustrate how the light of the Kingdom of God should not be hidden and should be made for all to see.

5   Many Jews were expecting a warrior Messiah; they expected to be released from the rule of Rome; when Jesus spoke about 'giving to Caesar what is Caesar's' he provoked a reaction of hate; the Pharisees were also against Jesus turning the tables in the Temple, as this undermined their authority there; 'turning the other cheek' when faced with confrontation was not a message of submission that many Jews wanted to hear; the charge of blasphemy allowed the Pharisees to present Jesus as a threat to Rome; being able to declare Him as a king provided the opportunity for crucifixion to take place.

6   c) 15

7   Women were effectively second-class citizens at the time, so would not have been listened to; men worked in a variety of places and associated with different types of people there; women mainly looked after the home; culturally, it would have been inappropriate for women to be disciples of a rabbi.

8   They were normal working men, so others would be able to connect with them; Jesus knew that by their nature, they were loyal and willing to follow; He could have called anyone – they were the first men He saw.

9   It illustrated the power of and the need to share the Word that He was bringing to the people and to the disciples; it revealed how people would react to the Word and encouraged the disciples to not lose faith when people chose to reject the Word; it emphasises the great rewards for those who hear the Word and act upon it; His listeners would have easily understood the agricultural aspects.

10 When Jesus rose from the dead, the disciples initially refused to believe; they rejected the words of Mary and the accounts of others; they couldn't believe until they met Jesus; this story can inspire Christians; this can show that lacking faith is not punished by God; the passage can reveal a sense of understanding from God that we sometimes need convincing; this does not give Christians the right to not believe; Jesus stated in Mark 16:16 that,

'Whoever believes and is baptised will be saved, but whoever does not believe will be condemned.'; many might feel it discouraging if even some of Jesus' closest friends, who had also seen miracles, could not believe it without seeing; some might find the word 'condemn' difficult to accept.

PAPER 3B – TEXTUAL STUDY: THE QUR'AN

Pages 231–234

1   a) Arabic

2   On a shelf; above all other books in the house.

3   It helps them to remember those Muslims who are not as well-off as they are and remind them of the importance of Zakah; allows Muslims to support each other on a daily basis, not just as a token gesture.

4   Learning Arabic allows a Muslim to read the Qur'an in its original language; this can provide a closer link to the text; the discipline of learning shows dedication to the faith; Allah may speak to the committed Muslim; many words and meanings can be lost in translation; the learning of Arabic allows the Muslim to understand the words that Muhammad recited.

5   The prophets before Muhammad helped to reveal the nature of Allah; through covenant and devotion, the prophets were able to prophesise what Muhammad was to reveal later; Ibrahim and Isa, for example, showed people what was to come and created a narrative for people to hold on to until the Qur'an was revealed; Muhammad was able to bring the teachings of all the other prophets together through the Qur'an; He was given the responsibility of this message and of being the last prophet of Islam; He is seen as the last prophet by many Muslims as the Qur'an cannot be changed or altered in any way; this would mean that no other prophets could now be included in it.

6   a) Surah

7   He showed great faith and commitment by building the Ark; he was saved by Allah because of his faithfulness and actions.

8   He was a key prophet of Allah but of lesser importance than Muhammad; he was trusted with prophecies that prepared the way for Muhammad and the receiving of the Qur'an.

9   Muhammad showed great devotion to Allah; he ensured he was close enough to Allah to receive the Qur'an from Him; as a role model, he shows the importance of listening to Allah; he also showed how this needs to happen over a long period of time, not just on occasion.

10 Muslims believe that they are judged in this life and at the end of this life; if they serve Allah in this life, He may see them prosper; this may be the blessing

of family or wealth or both; Allah rewards those who follow the teachings of the Qur'an and uphold the Five Pillars; after this life, Muslims will be judged and their eternity decided; following Allah allows passage into paradise; rejection of Allah can see an eternity of separation; Muslims are to follow Allah throughout life for His glory and not for their own gain; glorifying Him should have greater value than the hope of a good life or a blessed eternity; just because a Muslim may be suffering does not mean that Allah is displeased with them.

PAPER 4A – RELIGION, PHILOSOPHY AND ETHICS: RELATIONSHIPS AND FAMILY

Pages 235–237

1 b) Marriage
2 Helps to bring to families together; can help business growth; allows for growth in the religion through subsequent children; many believe it allows for a more suitable and beneficial match.
3 Marriage vows are made in the presence of God – the promises are made both spiritually and physically; they form part of a legal union which has responsibilities to be undertaken in law; they are a public declaration of promises pledged.
4 To show their love to each other; as a public sign of commitment; so that they can have sex in line with their religious beliefs; to provide a family foundation for their children.
5 Many would argue the value of civil partnerships; in the UK, many couples choose to live together as opposed to getting married; some couples feel as though they can't afford to get married but want to be together; around 50% of UK marriages end in divorce; religious believers would argue the value of a union before their god; they could also argue that it provides the best environment for bringing up children; marriage is still a declaration of love and commitment.

PAPER 4B – RELIGION, PHILOSOPHY AND ETHICS: EXISTENCE OF GOD

Pages 238–240

1 c) Omnibenevolent
2 Their family may already be believers; faith in God can give them hope beyond this life; they may have read the scriptures and found belief in them; they may have had a personal experience.
3 Many religious believers argue that if God wanted to be proven then He would already have done; we do not have the correct checks and experiments to 'test' for God; if God's existence was proven then there would be no need for faith and belief; others argue there is no God so the existence of God could never be proven.
4 The belief that God will end the world as we know it – will separate humanity; Jesus will be revealed to

all and Satan cast away from Him.
5 Too many religious views on God are similar; the stories give rise to the argument that they are made up; scriptures do not provide enough evidence to propose that their god is the true God; the rejection of Jesus by the Jews brings conflict between them and Christianity; religious believers would each argue that their god is the true God; they could point to life experience and scripture for evidence; interpretations of the same god would not automatically prove that there is no god; accepting that there is a god is an action of faith and not fact.

PAPER 4C – RELIGION, PHILOSOPHY AND ETHICS: PEACE AND CONFLICT

Pages 241–243

1 c) 30
2 Jesus taught that we should 'turn the other cheek'; they could follow the parable of the Good Samaritan; one of the Ten Commandments is 'do not kill'.
3 If a peaceful resolution can be found through talking then war can be avoided; diplomacy also costs a huge amount less than war and saves human and financial suffering.
4 Throughout history, religious believers have opposed the views of those who belong to different religions; there have been times when religious adherents have claimed land as their own, leading to conflict, e.g. the Crusades.
5 Holding nuclear weapons can deter a country from attacking another; nuclear weapons are unlikely to be used anyway; maintaining an arsenal would prevent nuclear scientists from working in other countries; the weaponry and its maintenance also provides jobs; nuclear weapons could fall into the wrong hands; civilians could lose their lives if nuclear weapons were used and the level of destruction would be impossible to justify; wars still happen despite countries holding nuclear weapons; their use is very unlikely so they are not a deterrent.

PAPER 4D – RELIGION, PHILOSOPHY AND ETHICS: CRIME AND PUNISHMENT

Pages 244–246

1 b) China
2 To help to protect society; to ensure that justice is served; to uphold the law; to change the offender for the better.
3 Should ensure that criminals don't reoffend in the future; is a cheaper alternative to having to keep imprisoning for repeat offences.
4 There have been too many people convicted of crimes they did not commit; the death penalty could be seen to contravene the Human Rights Act of 1998.
5 Victims of crime are considered through aims such

Answers

as restoration and restorative punishments; these punishments can also give confidence to the public in the justice system; many punishments of this nature could also act as deterrents; restorative justice, which seeks to help give the victim involvement and closure, is often seen to have a reformative impact on the offender; Islam allows for involvement of the victim, seeing it as a good deed in the eyes of Allah when compassion is shown; punishments could include paying for damage or replacing stolen items; these would not allow time to be spent rehabilitating criminals; the chances of re-offence would be high; there is every chance that a victim's views could be tainted by emotion; where there are multiple victims, it could be difficult to come to a conclusive punishment.

PAPER 4E – RELIGION, PHILOSOPHY AND ETHICS: HUMAN RIGHTS AND SOCIAL JUSTICE

Pages 247–249

1 a) Bullying
2 Christians are taught to treat each other as they would wish to be treated themselves; the Golden Rule shows that all should be treated equally.

3 He wanted to see equal rights for black Americans; he wanted to see an equal America for his children; being a Christian minister focused his beliefs on equality; as a Christian, he believed that all humans are created equal, and that Jesus stood up against the prejudices he witnessed, such as the treatment of the poor.
4 The law punishes acts of discrimination; punishment includes prison time as well as financial penalties; employment law includes ways in which jobs have to be made available to as many people as possible, without any discriminating factors coming into play.
5 If all people were treated equally, there would be no consequences for actions; criminals have to lose their rights because of their actions; children cannot be given the same freedoms as adults; disabled people may need extra support and will therefore be treated differently; treating people equally may not mean treating people the same; it could be argued that all people should receive the same basic rights, with certain enhancements; a religious believer may see each person as being a creation of their god; Christians are taught that all humans are made in God's image; if all people were treated the same, there would be less violence and poverty.

Notes

Notes

Notes

GCSE Religious Studies Workbook

Notes

ACKNOWLEDGEMENTS

The authors and publisher are grateful to the copyright holders for permission to use quoted materials and images.

P125 By jesario [GFDL (http://www.gnu.org/copyleft/fdl.html) or CC BY-SA 4.0-3.0-2.5-2.0-1.0 (http://creativecommons.org/licenses/by-sa/4.0-3.0-2.5-2.0-1.0)], via Wikimedia Commons

All other images are ©Shutterstock.com or © HarperCollinsPublishers Ltd.

Every effort has been made to trace copyright holders and obtain their permission for the use of copyright material. The authors and publisher will gladly receive information enabling them to rectify any error or omission in subsequent editions. All facts are correct at time of going to press.

Published by Collins
An imprint of HarperCollinsPublishers Ltd
1 London Bridge Street
London SE1 9GF

©HarperCollinsPublishers Limited 2020

ISBN 9780008166335

First published 2017
This edition published 2020

10 9 8 7 6

British Library Cataloguing in Publication Data.

A CIP record of this book is available from the British Library.

Commissioning Editor: Katherine Wilkinson
Authors: Dan Phillips and Rob Phillips
Project Leader: Richard Toms
Project Management: Donna Cole
Cover Design: Sarah Duxbury and Kevin Robbins
Inside Concept Design: Ian Wrigley
Text Design and Layout: Jouve India Private Limited
Production: Lyndsey Rogers and Paul Harding
Printed by: CPI Group (UK) Ltd, Croydon, CR0 4YY

MIX
Paper from
responsible source
FSC
www.fsc.org   FSC C007454

This book is produced from independently certified FSC™ paper to ensure responsible forest management.

For more information visit:
www.harpercollins.co.uk/green